Life in the Jetstream

10 Ways to Navigate and THRIVE in Turbulent Times

by Toni Thomas Durden

Life in the Jetstream, © 2014 by Toni Thomas Durden. All rights reserved.

No part of this book may be reproduced by any mechanical, photographic, or electronic process, or in the form of phonographic or audio recording: nor may be stored in a retrieval system, transmitted, or otherwise be copied for public or private use-other than "fair use" as brief quotation embodied in articles or reviews without prior permission of the publisher. All rights reserved for translation into foreign languages. No liability is assumed with respect to use of this information contained in this volume.

ISBN-13: 978-1508960416

Library of Congress Control Number: 2014953299

Printed in the United States of America

Result Driven Life Publishing

www.resultdrivenlifepublishing.com

Praise for Toni Thomas Durden

"It has been an awesome wonder to watch Toni rise above the worst of odds & succeed to such a high level over the last 11 years. There truly are NO EXCUSES and anything is possible when you learn from people who have carved out a simple formula to succeed. You are now holding that formula that worked for Toni and it WILL work for you!"

- Dani Johnson, Radio/TV host, best-selling author of *First Steps to Wealth* and *Spirit Driven Success*, international speaker who cares for thousands of orphans EVERY month.

"Writing a story that reveals your inner most secrets is a transparency beyond comprehension. Toni has pulled off the veil to look within so we can heal through her pain. Toni is the example of how resilient the human spirit can be. "

- Ana Maria Sanchez, best- selling author of *Girl from the Hood, Gone Good.*

"Toni has the rare gift of being able to dance in the rain. These pages will take you on a journey of self-reflection, allowing you new insights to your own personal stories. With the wisdom, heart, and humor unique to Toni, she will inspire you to dive into the next chapter of your life and love every second of it!"

- Ellen Bradley Ganus, author, speaker, and Multi-Million Dollar earner with a Health and Wellness Company

"Having known Toni for almost twenty-five years, I've watched a shy, timid young girl find her way. She blossomed into a strong, confident, woman who lets no obstacles stand in her way in order to pursue her dreams.

She is generous and compassionate with an amazing ability to connect others."

- Tom Kalili D.M.D, inventor, lecturer at UCLA, and Cosmetic Dentist in Beverly Hills, CA.

"Toni Durden has created an easy to understand guide that is intelligent, compassionate and filled with simplified "must haves" of life! Toni's honest stories about her own life struggles are shocking, humbling and incredibly inspiring! Familiar stories all of us can relate to. Durden shows us how not to just sleep with our dreams, but to wake up and chase them. This book is incredibly satisfying and will empower you beyond measure."

-Erik Betts, actor, stuntman, and speaker

Table of Contents

Dedication _____ 7
Acknowledgements _____ 8
Foreword _____ 12
Introduction _____ 15
Chapter 1 _____ 21
Chapter 2 _____ 26
Chapter 3 _____ 36
Chapter 4 _____ 48
Chapter 5 _____ 59
Chapter 6 _____ 83
Chapter 7 _____ 93
Chapter 8 _____ 139
Chapter 9 _____ 165
Chapter 10 _____ 199
Chapter 11 _____ 216
Chapter 12 _____ 236
Chapter 13 _____ 252
Chapter 14 _____ 268
Chapter 15 _____ 282

Dedication

I dedicate this book to my mom, Carol Turner. Thanks for NEVER giving up on us.

"And we know that God causes everything to work together for the good of those who love God and are called according to his purpose for them" (Romans 8:28)

You've called me a dreamer my entire life. I embraced it! Dreams really do come true!

Acknowledgements

I thank God for second, third, fourth, and fifth chances. You never gave up on me when you had every reason to. I give you ALL the honor and glory, for who I am and everything I do. It is because of you that I share my life with the world. You made me whole again. Jesus, your grace is ALWAYS sufficient. You gave me more than double for my trouble.

Rob, it has been twenty years together as my partner and husband. You have dealt with all of my shortcomings over the years. It has been a bumpy road, but thanks for helping me learn to communicate and not walking away when I couldn't speak. Although you didn't understand the burning desire I had to see this project through at first, you became my #1 fan. I love you more today than I ever have before. Learning to LOVE anyone else including myself was not easy; thanks for sticking it out. I look forward to the next twenty years together.

Austin and Kieran, I am blessed and grateful to have you in my world. Thank you for being supportive and understanding throughout this journey. You both are talented, handsome, caring, and compassionate young men.

May your road ahead be paved with whatever you need to have abundant, Godly lives. I love you dearly. I have done my best to help you understand not to judge a book by its cover and to see the best in everyone. We don't know what people have been through. Kesun, when you came into our life, we fell in love with you immediately. There is something special and unique inside you. We have our own story to tell. When you came into my life, it was a pivotal time for me. You still have the rest of your story to write. Helping you find your voice was important to me. You'll never know what an impact you made. Although we call you our "adopted son," you are more a part of this family than you'll know. We love you.

To my mom, thank you from the bottom of my heart for believing in me. Our story can bring healing. It's difficult to face our pain-filled past, but I'm grateful you are courageous enough to let God be God and do the work he intends to do. You helped me become a strong, independent, and spiritual woman.

JoAnne Lackey, my Nana, you changed my life at 13 years old when you walked into it. You were my rock, my mentor, my friend, and I miss you dearly. You helped me to believe in myself. You stood in my corner, without judgment, when I was trying to find myself. I will forever be grateful to you. My life wouldn't look the same without you in it.

I want to thank my mentor, Dani Johnson. I came to know you when I was hitting rock bottom. It took Kerri 7 years for me to meet you personally, for which I thank her even today. They say, when the student is ready the teacher will come. You challenged me emotionally, physically, financially, and spiritually. I'm humbled! God has given you an amazing gift, and I thank you for being so faithful. You're touching millions of lives. I will continue to sing your praises, because of what he's doing through you.

Thanks to Alicia Dunams from Bestseller in a Weekend. I needed the kick in the butt to finish what I started. This has been the most difficult, and yet the most rewarding, thing I've ever done. I would still be one of the "SOMEDAY" people had I not found you. Elizabeth, thanks for the phone calls, emails and questions answered as this process is difficult on the authors, but more challenging for you to see it through.

I also want to send out a big thank you to all my friends, family, and the people who came and went in my life. You have all helped me learn some of life's valuable lessons.

Thanks to the many authors of some of the most amazing books I've read who have contributed to restoring my purpose. I appreciate your stories of hope.

Those of you who have taken the time to read this book: I'm honored and humbled. I don't know you personally, but hope to get that opportunity someday soon. You inspire me to step up and continue to follow my heart. We, together, have the ability to change the world. I hope you continue the journey with me. I thank you from the bottom of my heart.

Foreword

Life is full of ups and downs. Often we find ourselves stumbling along a path we didn't choose. We encounter people we didn't anticipate meeting, in places we never imagined being. We plan, but planning doesn't prepare us for the unexpected. We trust that the path is right.

The randomness of the events that will ultimately shape our lives often appears to bring utter chaos in the moment. We all wish for the easy life filled will joy, but it is when we are working through the difficult times that we experience the most personal growth. Those moments define who we are and give us greater insight to our life's purpose on Earth.

If you are willing to be patient, mindful, and resilient through these challenging times, you can accomplish things that will amaze others and most importantly, surprise yourself.

We all need help. It is important to give but equally important to receive. No one is going to make it through this life alone; we must be willing to ask and receive help. Toni is sharing her personal experiences to show us the many issues that unfolded in her life and how she learned from them. Learning how others overcome difficult times can help us empower ourselves, transform our lives, and wake us up to a new reality.

We all want the fairytale ending, to live happily ever after. The movies distort our perception. In "Movie Land," all this self-discovery and change takes place in 90 minutes. Don't let that discourage you. The story of our lives is constantly being rewritten by the choices we make every day. As an actor, I have always been a dreamer. Dreaming and fantasy are wonderful tools for escaping reality, but it is DOING and taking action that has allowed me to overcome the various struggles with my career, my relationships, loss of loved ones, and all the life-changing moments. No matter who you are, we all live with the uncertainty of change. Don't let the fear of the unknown debilitate you, and don't compare yourself to others. The grass always seems greener on the other side, but maybe we just need to water ours a little more. Just do the work; it will make all the difference.

To complete a project like this takes courage, determination, perseverance, passion, and a true desire to help others. Toni shares her experiences with a genuine and open heart; without fear of judgment. The vulnerability shared in this book will inspire you, give you hope, and ignite a sense of urgency to take action.

We have the power to choose where life takes us, even when we've diverted off course. It's time to start really living and doing something that matters. Prioritize what is important in your life today. Live today as if it were your last.

- Andrew St. John

Introduction

Life is like an international flight to NOWHERE, but, my reservation was to Paradise. Think about what happens when you plan to go on a vacation? You are excited with anticipation, the planning begins. You set a date, a destination, decide how long you'll be there, make a reservation, choose a hotel you'll be staying at, what transportation you'll use, things you'll do when you're there, among the many other decisions you'll make. What happens when you're preparing for the trip? You are motivated and driven to reach that goal, and make it to your destination.

You pack your bags only to find out that a wheel on your suitcase is broken. You can't seem to find your reservation, and then your car decides to go on the fritz on the way to the airport. You go through security and get chosen for the pat down. They riffle through your luggage and take your toothpaste. You make it to the gate only to find out you have a two-hour delay due to a weather problem, which will make you miss your connecting flight. You finally board the plane and get a middle seat next to a mother with a screaming infant on her lap. When you arrive, you're exhausted and now have to pay for your own hotel

Life in the Jetstream

because it wasn't the airline's problem, it was Mother Nature's. Something so exciting loses its luster in a short period of time once reality sets in, and the start of your trip is not turning out to be what you expected. How does that happen?

Our lives work in a similar way. However, there is a major difference. Most of us rarely have a destination to start with. We are flying blind, and hoping to make it to paradise. We will only make it to paradise if we commit to the plan, ANY plan. If you're not specific in what you WANT, you'll definitely NEVER get there. You will choose a life by default, when you could have designed it all along. We are all handed a different set of circumstances and lots of problems that we don't understand. Some of us may be depressed, bitter, or angry about what's been thrown our way. It may even stop some of us in our tracks. You may even decide the trip is just NOT worth it. Your flight plan is how life unfolds for you. The question is "Where is your next destination?"

Books are an escape in my so-called adventure. However, I found that most books seem to be focused on only one subject. We have three-dimensional lives with our MIND, BODY, and SPIRIT, so of course we all will have

Introduction

multiple issues. Our goal is to become balanced in all aspects of our lives. What if someone doesn't know where to begin? It's time to assess your life and current situation to see where you are.

Living life in the jetstream is my personal journey, complete with the peaks and valleys we go through when we wake up every day in this thing called "LIFE." It's about learning lessons along the way, through the turbulence and struggles we all face. Many of us choose to be victims of circumstance. Why is that? It's easier not to step up. Our individual woe-is-me story allows us to make as many excuses as we'd like without taking the responsibility to move on. I'm not an exception by any means. I've done some unthinkable things. I'm human, learning everyday just like the rest of you. My twenty-five year flying career has helped me understand that we can't be in control of everything, no matter how hard we try. I find we are happier when we can let go of some of our expectations.

Some of us are not in the right place at the right time. We have dysfunctional lives. We are raised by single or absentee parents. What is dysfunction, by the way? I think that in this day and time, all of us can say we live with some sort of dysfunction, whatever you think is not normal. We don't have enough money or we have too much. We are overweight or underweight. We are abused or mistreated. We are not given enough attention or we are given too much. We all have a story to tell. Our stories should be about personal growth, healing, and how we can relate so we can help others. It is a continuous process. I believe it empowers all of us to look at our own lives and realize so many other people have it so much worse than we do.

What I have found is that many people want to remain anonymous with their past. Some are not ready to share their story because they have not quite arrived where they want to be. They haven't resolved some of their issues. On the other side of the spectrum, there are those like myself, who want to SHOUT it from the mountaintop because we know healing comes from acknowledging and overcoming our past, then, healing can begin. My goal is for you to take the NEXT step forward, toward a positive change in your life. Get the results you have always dreamed of. If you have forgotten your dream, maybe this will inspire you to find a new one. My life lessons will hopefully help you make better decisions than I did. I want you to THRIVE despite the old baggage you're carrying around.

Introduction

I have been faced with alcoholism, drugs, sexual abuse, bullying, rape, suicide, murder, and financial ruin, among many other issues. I couldn't afford a counselor, so reading helped me get through the psychological issues I wanted to put behind me. I am delighted and thrilled that you have taken a chance on me as I share my journey. I pray you are open-minded and non- judgmental. I want to be as candid as possible with you, as writing this book has truly been a healing ground for me. Every day is a new day. Like an alcoholic who is first starting AA, we all face daily tasks and decisions that must be completed and made as we begin living a life of freedom. It's NOT easy. Don't expect it to be. You can't read one book or go to one meeting and all of the sudden you're a new person. This process is a series of stepping stones.

You deserve to be happy, prosperous, and fulfilled. My new motto is: "Why dream, because reality can't really be this good." Your choices can create the life that dreams are made of. You have the opportunity to write a new chapter. If you didn't like the cards you were dealt, then change them.

I will share my tragedies as well as my triumphs. It's a starter kit to recognizing your life's lessons. It's your movie

Life in the Jetstream

to produce: you control the scenes, the characters, and most importantly, you decide how it ends. It's not about how you get your start in life; it's about how you finish. I hope to make this a pleasurable experience for you. Sit back, relax, and enjoy the ride in the friendly skies.

Chapter 1

(Prepare for Take-off)
In the Beginning…. How it All Began

WHAT'S IN A NAME? MY NAME IS TONI THOMAS. My name came in a unique way, but let me share with you briefly what happened prior to my arrival in this world. Discovering part of my history gave me insight to what lies ahead. My mother was born with 4 other siblings. She and her sister had been sent to live with her grandmother as babies. She only lived with her biological mother from 5 to 6 years old. She did not have a close relationship with her mother or father. My mother only remembers getting a few visits from her biological father when she was about 12. He only came around when he was forced to pay child support. She loved the little bit of attention she did get during that time. She remembers he bought her a doll and a plastic necklace during one of his visits. She felt like a princess for that short period of time. Her sister had a different father and was jealous of the rare visits and the few gifts my mother received. This was the start of some bitterness between the siblings.

Her grandmother raised her in a small town called Cola, where there was barely enough food to be had. Times were extremely difficult back then. My mother was looking for a way out of her living situation, so she chose to get married at 15 years old. Forget living in a trailer park she lived on a bus, and not a traveling one, with her new husband. She dropped out of school in the tenth grade. My biological father was in the army and had a love of music. She gave birth to my oldest brother at the age of 17 when she was merely a child herself.

The year my mother quit school, she had watched a local school pageant. The girl who won was named Toni Thomas. My mother was enamored by the beauty and grace of this girl. She said that if she ever had a girl, her name would be Toni. She so happened to marry a man with the last name of Thomas. What a coincidence! I had two older brothers, one year apart from each other. My mom had three of us by the age of 19. My biological father was a raging alcoholic, and later he was dishonorably discharged from the military. He played in a rock and roll band, drank all night, and would sneak back into the house in the wee hours of the night. He was violent during his drunken rants and beat my mother. He was a womanizer and couldn't care less that he had a wife and children to come home to. The odds weren't very good for my mother's start in life. The story only begins with my mom getting divorced at 20.

Chapter 1

My birth father never had any part of my life. I probably have only seen him about ten times over the years, that I can remember. We left North Carolina and moved to Florida for a new beginning. I really don't recall many childhood events other than moving, A LOT! A few of our family members let us live with them until their landlords started forcing us to leave. We lived in a station wagon. This was my mom's first car and she paid $75 for it. We showered at our cousin's house from time to time. My mom worked multiple jobs and was absent most of the time, as she tried to put food on the table for us.

My brothers and I walked home from school quite often. It was a scenic route; over the bridge was the ocean as far as the eye could see. We would even walk to Sambo's (a local restaurant similar to Denny's), where my mom worked. We walked home from school on the sidewalks over major bridges and main intersections. I look back now and can't even imagine letting my children do that. My brothers and I were about 7, 8, and 9 years old. In the last few years, I have visited the town of Venice more often. I'm still shocked to see how far everything truly is. My mom always said God helped her through raising us, because she certainly didn't have a clue. Today, I look back and think how lucky we truly were.

I remember my favorite teacher in kindergarten was Ms. Madison. I started at 4 years old and had a zest for life. I was recently reading a newspaper clipping I found during Christmas of 1973. Evidently, a reporter came to my class because Santa was coming for a visit. They said I gathered up all the timid children and wanted to make sure they told Santa what they wanted for Christmas. I would ask again and again, "Did you get that?" I found a few of my classmates hadn't had a turn and moved them closer to Santa. The reporter said "that I was obviously going to be in the public relations field because I had started so early." I guess there was some insight to whom or what I would later become. There is nothing better than having that childlike faith. You can be ANYBODY, conquer ANYTHING before life starts to hand you some lemons.

Ask Yourself:

Have you had situations in your life when you felt trapped with no way out? Have you searched for attention from a father or mother that was always absent? Have you gone hungry in your life? Have you been tossed to the side as if nobody cared, and now you have abandonment issues? Did you get a bad start in life and don't feel like you can turn it around?

Chapter 1

Life's Lessons:

I can elaborate in later sections about wanting to GET OUT of my personal situations. When we have been denied a relationship with our fathers, emotional issues will become apparent. You may have had a father who was at home but wasn't present in your daily life. This too will affect you. You will be searching to please and get the attention you need. I wasn't any different than most. No matter how you get started in life, you can still have all of your desires. You can have a fresh start! I started going to church at an early age and learned of another kind of Father. I needed a father whom I can depend on and rely on. He would be there for me in good times and in bad. I couldn't see him, but I knew he was there. He became my imaginary friend.

Chapter 2

(Severe Turbulence)
Innocence Lost

WHILE LIVING IN FLORIDA, MY MOM WORKED DAY AND NIGHT TO PROVIDE a roof over our head, food to eat, and clothes on our back. We had people who would take us in and help us out from time to time, who then became friends of the family. I do remember some fond memories being with that family. Grandma B had a horse named Ginger. I loved her so much. I always thought she was rich because she could afford a horse. It was rare, but I did get to ride her every now and then. This gave me a true love for horses. It also gave me another dream, to have a horse of my own one day.

As a child, the main memories I can recall were not something a child should ever have to go through. A friend of the family let us stay with them while my mom worked. Grandma B also had a 16-year-old son at the time. His mother was trying to be helpful by giving us a place to go, but in turn, it was the beginning of my long road of healing ahead. It's so unfortunate, that this 16-year-old stole my innocence. I had to learn how to make sense of the unthinkable. Here's a 16-year-old boy taking advantage of

Chapter 2

baby girls. Yes, I did find out later in life that I was not the only one, that there were many more. I'll share in a later chapter when the abuse surfaced for me again. I thought I had put it behind me, but it decided to rear its ugly head once again.

I was sexually abused starting at the age of six. I look back today and ask how we can learn from this. I have asked my family members how they didn't see the signs. I wasn't blaming them, but wanted to recognize red flags when they popped up. I was the baby, yet I always went to bed later then my older brothers when we stayed at their house. My abuser always wanted me to sit on his lap. I asked my mom, "Did I act any different around him?" She has no recollection of me being afraid of him. You play the scenes over and over in your head as if you'll find out that something was wrong with you. What did I do? Why didn't I tell someone?

If you have been abused and have never talked about it, you need to find a trusted friend and or deal with it through counseling. You will always feel dirty, unworthy, and hopeless. You'll believe it's your fault until these issues get resolved. You will act out your behaviors and do things you don't want to because you already feel USED! It doesn't have to be that way. You have the ability to get your life back and become whole again. Over and over again, this dirty little secret will eat at you every day of your life. As you'll read, I did so many silly things I wish I could take back, now that I know WHO I am. It was all about my journey to find myself. Don't get me wrong; I'm still vulnerable and I still make bad choices, but I take the time to process how I think and feel about a situation now.

There are so many circumstances that I put myself in, up through my adult years. I was always wondering, "'HOW could I be so naïve?" I always want to trust until I am given a reason not to. I want to see the best in everyone because I know from the bottom of my heart, there IS good in all of us. I have found that those who are hurting others in some way are acting out their misfortunes done to them. I won't say ALL, but for the most part, that is certainly accurate. Bullies keep bullying because they have been bullied; abusers abuse in most cases because they have been abused.

There is NO excuse for abuse of ANY kind. It is NOT acceptable. In today's society, we are numb because of what we see on TV and in the movies. Our concerns and our abuse are written off, as if they're NOT that bad. If you

Chapter 2

have ever been touched inappropriately at any time, you have reason to be alarmed. I was absolutely floored when I was discussing my abuse with someone and they had the nerve to say, "If he didn't penetrate with his private parts it's not abuse." WHAT? Are you kidding me? I'm not the violent type, but I could have strangled this person at that moment. I was a 6-year-old girl getting violated in every other way, doing and seeing unspeakable things a little girl should have never been exposed to. It's demeaning and shameful to have people disregard what you value.

Sexual abuse is a power where the offender controls the victim and the sexual encounter is not mutually conceived. Someone in power or authority orders you to do sexual acts, and you are manipulated, intimidated, or forced to comply. The knowledge is when the offender understands the significance and implication of the sexual encounter. They tend to be older and more intelligent than the victim. Then you have the gratification offenders, who participate to gratify themselves by what they are doing to the victim or having the victim do to them. You have non-contact acts of abuse and actual sexual contact. It's all abuse! You can read all about the differences and what constitutes abuse at www.childwelfare.gov. Do you know how often sexual abuse occurs? One in four is affected by sexual abuse. It

29

needs to stop!

During this time of abuse, I was in first grade. I knew we didn't have much, and I'm sure it could have been much worse. As an adult, I often look back and say we could have been put in foster homes or my mom could have been a drug addict who left us for days at a time. There are so many worse situations. Watching my mom let us eat while she went hungry, gave me the understanding of what unconditional love really is. As children, we don't realize the sacrifices parents make for us until one day we become the parent.

I remember being so scared watching my mom drive through the night trying to stay awake, her back hurting as she leaned over the steering wheel. She would ask if I'd rub her back for a minute. I thought she was going to fall asleep and we would wreck. She was basically comatose when at home after working several jobs trying to support us. She didn't know what welfare was and was glad that she did what she had to without the governments help. She wasn't looking for a free ride; she was willing to work. She worked so much her goal was basically to provide for us. Even though it meant living in survival mode for years to come. These memories will forever be ingrained in my

Chapter 2

mind.

Growing up, I was a bit chubby, or so I was told. That also didn't help with my self-esteem. I can still hear the name-calling of "Toni Bologna Meatball eyes put her in the oven and make French fries" and "Butterball." However, when I look back at old photos, I don't seem to have been that fat. I don't know why I was tormented for so long. That psychologically changed me over the years. For years I said, "I was destined to be fat because most of my family was overweight." I guess I was being prepared for all the battles I would eventually face ahead.

Remember, your perception is different from someone else's reality. I learned this lesson over and over again. You can grow up in the same household with the same family and everyone has a different experience. That has nothing to do with being good or bad, but it is YOUR reality. It's no fault of anyone how they see events as they unfold. However, it can be devastating and life changing to those who feel they have been violated, mistreated, abandoned, or written off as being over dramatic.

In second grade, I started acting out. I had asked my mom for a long time to take me to the stables to see the

31

horses. It was about five miles away. She never got around to it due to her work schedule, and I finally got tired of waiting. Let me remind you, I was in second grade. I made a plan and skipped school. I skipped school, really… What 7-year-old skips school? I got up, got ready for school and acted as if I were getting on the bus. I hid behind the bushes until the bus took off and I started my five-mile walk through the back woods. What could I be thinking? I wanted to go so badly. I just had to do it.

I finally made it to the stable and there was a man working. He was cleaning the stalls. I got up close looking at the horses, and he invited me in. He did ask if my parents knew where I was. I don't remember my answer, but his facial expression was disbelief. I guess I said yes, my mom knew where I was. He never led on and asked me if I wanted to help around the farm. Yes, of course, I said.

We brushed the horses, scooped the poop, filled the water troughs, and we fixed the fence. At lunch, a woman I suppose was his wife fixed us a sandwich and a soda. I do remember asking him the time pretty often. I was trying to time it right to walk the five miles back and beat the bus. Well, I didn't make it. I was late, about 30 minutes to an hour late. I made it back to my street and what I saw ahead

Chapter 2

seemed like an AMBER ALERT was flashing. I was the MISSING person. Police were everywhere. Boy, did I dread walking back through my door.

As I walked up the street I could see a lot of commotion going on at my house. The police were there; neighbors and friends were around. I knew I had messed up big time! I kept on walking because I couldn't think of anything to say, other than, what really happened. I decided to face the music. I could see my mom was embarrassed when I explained what I did. Everyone started leaving when they realized that I was fine. Every time mom tried to give me a spanking, someone else would show up at the house or the phone would ring. I remember thinking, "let the interruptions keep coming." I did end up getting a much-deserved whipping with the belt. This was how my mom showed me she was serious. It was a serious issue.

After this incident my mother had the foresight to try getting me help. She contacted Big Brothers Big Sisters of South Sarasota County, and I was given my first big sister. I was afraid to have a friendship with her, I didn't realize why at the time. So they gave me another sister. She was younger, and I thought I could relate. I was going to be a good girl and talk to her so I didn't lose her to. Her name

Life in the Jetstream

was Debbie. I have to say that she made my world a bit better and brighter. We would go to the park, have lunch, and sit at the beach. She brought me small gifts, and it was a change I really needed at the time. I was able to talk to her, but still hesitant. I needed a mentor, yet it was hard for me to trust anyone. We did have several good times. Unfortunately, a change was coming faster than I knew. I was going to have to say good-bye to someone I just learned to love and trust.

Ask Yourself:

Have you ever felt like the fat kid? Have you done silly things that you wished you hadn't? Have you been exposed to inappropriate behavior? Did you see yourself once as hopeful and now seem hopeless? Have you ever acted out and not realized why?

Life's Lessons:

I felt like the fat kid because of what people said about me. People will call you names and mistreat you the rest of your life. Choose not to accept what they say and know your TRUTH. We cannot expect others to encourage us and pat us on the back before we are able to feel good about ourselves. We all make mistakes growing up. The idea is to learn from them so we don't repeat them. If you have been abused, don't wait get help now. The longer you put it off, the more emotional trauma you will suffer. You will continue to make bad decisions, and it will be a long time before you can look in the mirror and LOVE YOURSELF. You can forgive yourself for all the things you have done. Learning to love yourself after suffering abuse and mistreatment will be a process. Stay the course. Don't beat yourself up. Children are influenced by movies, music, and especially YOU! Help them create a safe place to communicate openly.

Chapter 3

(Diversion Ahead)
Making the Move, Life with More Uncertainty

THERE IS A POSITIVE LESSON IN EVERYTHING. What doesn't kill you WILL make you stronger. Let me back up a bit. We moved to Virginia from Venice, Florida in 1978. My mom's aunt and uncle came to help us move. We would live with them until my mom could get on her feet. Once again, we moved in with another family. I thought they were rich, too. They lived in a BIG house and had three daughters. I do remember eating a lot of potato soup there. We lived in the basement of their house. I was like, "WOW they have two full houses, an upstairs and downstairs." It's kind of comical now because I had never seen a basement.

My uncle owned a tobacco farm. All of us would head to the fields and work the farm on the weekends. My brothers got to ride the tractor and my job was to pick suckers off the tobacco. Those felt like long grueling days, but we were happy to have a break for lunch, when I could eat my favorite meal, a hotdog and a soda of my choice. We didn't get to eat out, so that was a nice surprise. We were all very sticky and dirty at the end of the day. I can't

Chapter 3

say I enjoyed it back then, but I'm grateful for the few times we did it. It made me realize I didn't want any hard labor jobs. It definitely can build character in kids today. Some kids have never washed dishes by hand, hung clothes out on the line or cut firewood. You know where I'm going with that. I appreciate that experience.

We had a great time in the evenings of some of those weekends. My aunt would come downstairs with the family to play the piano and let us sing Christian music. My favorite song was "Behold the Lamb." My cousin Sherry and I would sing the song from the top of our lungs. They had a beautiful fireplace. We'd sit around and just watch the glow. Sherry and I use to play Wonder Woman and make mud pies. I felt like a kid again. Finally, mom was working at another Sambo's in Collinsville and was able to move us into our NEW home. For some reason, I believe the price was twenty-eight thousand dollars. Why I even cared, I don't know. It was a lot of money back then though. She had a few of the male employees come take down the brush, mow the lawn, and help clean the house to get us set up. I loved to see people come to help, yet they weren't getting anything in return. Does this really even happen anymore?

37

Life in the Jetstream

My mom struggled to pay the bills. Many times when she couldn't afford oil for the heat in the winter, she would hang up blankets on the doorway by the kitchen and open the stove so we could get warm. We lived about 3 or 4 miles from our elementary school and were only a 10 minute walk from our high school. We would take the bus in the winter and walk home in the warmer months.

Mom worked the late shift, so my brothers and I would run and jump in the bed in my brother's room so we weren't scared of being home alone. My mom was reported to social services, with neighbors saying we were asking for food at other peoples' houses and running around the neighborhood unattended. That was another uncertain time for us.

We didn't really know what was going on, but could see how it stressed my mom out. She scurried to find affordable babysitters. They were all the same. They would talk to their boyfriends on the phone and didn't really pay much attention to us. The boyfriends would stop by and say "Hi" to pass the time. It's amazing what kids pick up because everyone that comes into your life influences you in some way. It could be a positive or negative experience. I was excited to have sitters come over only to realize that

Chapter 3

they weren't interested in being there. They had other things on their minds.

In 1980, my mom met a man who would later become my step-dad. They started dating, and before my mom remarried, she thought it would be a good idea for us (the children) to call the new man in her life "DAD." I was angry because I did not want to call someone DAD, unless he had earned it. I was rebellious in many ways and understandably so. He was very strict. He also had a son and a daughter as well. I felt my world was being turned upside down again.

They married in April 1981. I had so many thoughts go through my head. My mom seemed happy, and I guess the marriage allowed her to relax a bit. She always carried the weight of the world on her shoulders. For her sake, I hoped she had gotten what she wanted. I did like having a sister for a short time. I wanted someone to talk to. His daughter moved in with us, and so did his son briefly. Not completely sure what happened, but I believe Dad was too strict and his son decided to go live with his mother.

In the beginning of the relationship, Dad's daily routine was getting up for morning coffee and reading the newspaper after my brothers and I went to school. He worked from 3 to 11 p.m. for many years at a cardboard factory. He would come home at 11:30 p.m. and start drinking his Canadian Mist and Mountain Dew. My mom was a manager of a well-known fast food chain by then. She worked many late nights, coming home about 1:30 a.m. When the house wasn't clean, my dad would drink and stew till my mom got home. He would then start a fight with her soon after. He would sometimes make her wake us up to clean the house when she arrived.

The fights became more severe as the years went on. Most of the fights were over the kids. My middle brother ate too much. They thought he had ring worm. They took him to the doctor to find out he was only a growing boy. He may have eaten out of boredom sometimes, but had no true health issue.

The arguments throughout my adolescence were unbearable. My dad would punch holes in the walls, break glasses or the coffee table, and threaten to kill either himself or my mom. Sometimes I would lie in my bed, praying my mother would stop arguing with him and just go to bed. This torment lasted until I graduated. We lived with this secret and pretended that everything was fine. He was an alcoholic and came with a lot of baggage from his past.

When I was about 12 years old, I was sleeping in my own room. I had years of suppressed memories of the abuse that happened. This night it will all come back to me. My dad came into my room three times after he'd been drinking. The first time, I was in a dead sleep and must have moved when he was by my bed. The second time, I woke up while he was touching me in an inappropriate place, and I began to sit up immediately as he hurried out of the room. I was so afraid that I couldn't go to sleep. He walked to my door again and stood there. I sat up in the bed so he knew I was wide awake. When I knew he went back to watch TV, I ran to my step-sister's room. I told her what actually happened and that I was afraid. I asked if I could I stay with her.

I was torn apart. I began having flashbacks of my past experiences, which had started at such an early age. I didn't know what to do, but I did know my abuse started just like this. I would rather have died than go through that again. I wanted to run away but had NOWHERE to go. I wanted to SCREAM, and CRY because I felt completely desperate. I was just a kid, a girl wanting to be NORMAL, whatever

Life in the Jetstream

that was.

I use to get extremely nauseous, holding back my anger and tears. I feel like that little girl, as if those memories of abuse were happening all over again. This was a FIGHT I could not win. There were NO winners here. Do I say something? Will she believe me? Was I going to tear apart this family? Was I going to stress my mom out? What should I DO? I kept hearing: it's your fault! Don't be selfish. It's all about you. You're a baby. I stayed up all night trying to reason with myself. Remember, nobody knew about any past abuse. We didn't talk about these things.

The next day changed my life forever. I went to school but was overwhelmingly emotional. I did not want to tell my mother. I did not know what her reaction would be. I didn't know what the end result would be, which made me hesitate. However, it changed the course of my future. I could not bear to stay quiet. Dying was an option at this point. I would kill myself if I had to tolerate the abuse again. Can you imagine committing suicide and not one person know why you did it. It could only get worse if I didn't do something. Who knows what else would happen. I needed to see what she would say or do, so I called her at

Chapter 3

work. Even though I know I didn't want to ruin her life.

She came and picked me up at school. I explained to her what had happened the night before. She decided to sit me in front of my step-father before he went to work, asking him "what he was doing in my room the night before." He replied, "I was tucking her in." I don't remember her reaction other than seemingly being satisfied or "relieved" with the answer. I guess he didn't want to tuck in the other three children that night.

That may seem uneventful to you, but that was a pivotal moment for me. I felt bad for my mom because of her struggles and what she had to give up for my brothers and me to stay together. All of that changed. That day, I HATED my mother. Those are strong words to use, but I knew at that point, I could NEVER depend on ANYBODY but myself. I made several vows. I would NEVER, EVER depend on a MAN to take care of me! This was a huge, defining moment of my life. I couldn't even describe what those feelings were until this day.

After moving from Florida to Virginia, I remember asking myself: "What are feelings? Did I have them? Do they exist? The basic needs of love and nurturing were non-

43

existent in my life, so did I get mad or sad? I didn't understand hope either. My skin later became thick like rhinoceros skin. It became thick and strong so that I could stay guarded and protected.

After that incident, you could cut the tension in the house with a knife. My brothers had no idea what had even happened. I merely existed. I got into several fist fights at school. I was a tomboy. Many incidents happened with my step-father's daughter during her 11th grade year, and she too decided to move back with her mom. So most of the fights mom and dad got into were about ME! I became the trouble-maker. Dad would jump all over my mother to beat me for the things I did wrong. He wanted to stand in my doorway and watch. Unfortunately, I egged it on for my mom to hit me harder because I wouldn't cry in front of her. He didn't need to lay a hand on me after this. Mom always tried to make-up for what happened to me and I don't think she ever even realized that's what she was doing.

How do you live a daily existence after this stuff happens? I can't say I share many fond memories of the past. As a family, we didn't go on many vacations. I do remember the few we had. We went to Florida to visit my family again. We also went to South Carolina to visit my

Chapter 3

dad's estranged family. We took a few beach trips and went to Carawind's Amusement Park. I realize now what you don't know growing up doesn't hurt you.

I do believe that if dad hadn't been so strict with me over the years, I would have probably ended up pregnant and maybe on welfare in my late teens. I was searching for love anywhere I could find it. I wouldn't have devoted so much time to myself the way I have. I wouldn't have invested into my first property at 19 to have something to show for the money I made. Although it was a bad situation for me, there were other positives that helped me become who I am today. Life is not about placing blame on others, it's about learning the lessons to make you a better person. It is also about seeing the bigger picture.

Ask Yourself:

Have you ever judged a book by its cover? Have you felt betrayed by someone you know and love? Have you thought about where you learned your core values and morals? Have you thought about suicide? Have you made vows and judgments you now regret? Has life handed you some rotten apples? Are you using the challenges you face as a way to grow? Do you still struggle with relationships with your family?

Life's Lessons:

My mom and dad had extremely horrific pasts. They were both given away, causing abandonment issues. They were both abused and got married at such a young age. They didn't have any resources to help them out of their situations. My mother was finally out of survival mode from all those earlier years. Let me say this, there is ABSOLUTELY NO EXCUSE for abuse of any kind. It is wrong and should be dealt with. Sometimes we need to look at all the information instead of just feeling victimized. It's easy to place blame on others, but the freedom is in understanding the circumstances.

Also, when you make vows like "never" and "always," you live with those vows for the rest of your life. I remained independent for all the future years to come. I would NOT allow a man to EVER "take care of me." I didn't TRUST them. You'll see later in my personal relationships why I had trouble.

Suicide should NOT be an option. There are so many places to get help and so many people willing to see you live an amazing life, despite the obstacles you'll face. Don't let what someone says or does control your life.

Chapter 3

As a child we are looking for someone to guide, protect, and validate our feelings. We don't want to be judged, accused, beat, ignored, criticized, or yelled at. You don't have to "fix us," sometimes we are just looking for a sounding board.

Chapter 4

(Put On Your Oxygen Mask, Sit Down and Hold On)
Building Character

MY BROTHER HAD A FRIEND FROM SCHOOL, and later my mother became friends with his mother. We went to their house one day to pick my brother up. I was a tomboy from the word go. I remember thinking, "WOW they must have MONEY!" They had a big house, nice cars, and good jobs. It was unbelievable! I was meeting his mother for the first time. It was a memorable day that will be embedded in my head forever. It was an awesome visit. I guess everyone was considered RICH compared to what I was familiar with. Why do kids even put a tag like being RICH on something? Believe it or not, I hear it from kids all the time today. I would rather them see that anything is possible for those who believe in their dreams.

This lady had such class and elegance. She was soft-spoken. I remember walking out the door to leave after having a good time. I yelled at my brother, "YOU DOGFACE!" She gasped as if I just cursed him out. She said to me, "young ladies don't talk like that." I was

Chapter 4

embarrassed. I had never heard such thing. This women came into my life and has been an inspiration to me ever since. She afforded me the opportunity to build my self-esteem and confidence. She helped put me in pageants to learn that there is more to life. She bought me clothes, took photos of me, and always made me feel like a princess. She helped make me the women I am today. I owe her so much that I'll never be able to repay.

I started doing school pageants in the 8th grade. These pageants raised money for the Boosters Club (sports teams) I won 3rd runner-up every year plus Miss Congeniality in the 10th grade. Wow! Miss Congeniality, what's that? You are selected by the contestants as having the best personality or being the most-liked. My Nana, JoAnne Lackey wanted me to branch out and try other pageant systems to help with my speech writing, interviewing with adults, and learning how to be an ambassador of good will. I was fortunate to have numerous wins and only a few losses. It certainly helped build my character. I learned what other girls were doing all over the U.S. It made me hungry for more. I did not like the dog-eat-dog competition or the mothers that acted like drooling vicious animals ready to bite at any minute.

It was also during this time that I was being taunted and bullied at school. I loved choir, but hated the ridicule from the other girls. I guess the bullying started when I was in 9th grade. I was in the auditorium for a school program and a girl decided it would be funny to "burn" my hair. We ended up in the principal's office and she did get suspended for THREE days. What a crime, what justice? We should not have had to worry about our kids going to school and someone burning their hair. Today, we have to worry about guns and knives.

I always liked to dress up for school. It made it easier for me not to get laughed at. I never had name-brand clothes to wear. I was made fun of for my hand-me-downs. I would get pushed around and the girls were just waiting to see if I would do anything about it. I was trying to learn how to be a lady. I spent many years being a tomboy up until 7th grade. I wanted desperately to change. Luckily, with my new experiences in pageants, I prayed the time would come sooner than later.

I have had just about everything happen to me in the "SPIRIT" of competition. I've had people tearing my clothes, stealing my belongings, and saying, "I'm just lucky." Mothers have booed at me so loud to drown out my

Chapter 4

singing during a competition. It can be cruel. I always had to hold my mother back from acting like the others. She didn't want to see me hurt. I wanted to be better than that. I would always try to take the high road.

I was 15 when, finally, my mother first told me she loved me. I didn't even know what that meant. I needed her to say that my entire life, but it came a little too late. I know she did the best she could do at the time. I needed a protector and to be nurtured. How can a mother meet such expectations? Especially when she was never equipped with the tools she needed to make better decisions. My mother was never told she was loved either. How could she possibly know? The choices I made later in life were because of this very reason. We try to find LOVE in all the wrong places, when you don't know what it means or how to show it.

My favorite part of the pageant system was getting a new outfit or gown. We didn't have much money, but this served as an escape for me. I could DREAM with the spotlight on me for about 30 seconds. I was a STAR in my own world. I didn't care whether I won or lost because I was still the winner in the end. This was my time that no one could take away. My world became bigger. I was

Life in the Jetstream

coming closer to amounting to "SOMEBODY." Despite my past, I was going to make a name for myself.

I had the fortunate opportunity to model for Vekeshia Designs and Looker's Modeling Agency. I loved doing runway shows in our local malls and nightclubs in Roanoke. My cousin, Sherry and I took a job teaching young girls how to walk the runway, as well as teaching proper etiquette, and basic modeling techniques. I was able to do a Billboard advertisement for DuPont while wearing Hanes hosiery. DuPont invited me to view their plant and show me around. It was quite interesting how things were made. It was also one of the most well-known factories in our area.

At school, I didn't get selected for many groups. I didn't get picked to be a cheerleader, flag squad, or even homecoming queen in high school. I have been non-traditional most of my life. I did gymnastics, track, Cavalier Singers but I was most proud of my competitive speed skating. I worked hard. There weren't high school distractions to slow me down. I excelled. I was great off the starting blocks, yet my endurance was less desirable to say the least. However, I found a relay partner who I worked well with. Tina had the endurance; I had the speed. We were a great team. I was proud of the awards we won through speed skating because that showed our team and individual efforts.

The skating rink was my home away from home. I was there every Wednesday, Saturday, and Sunday. I had many lessons that I learned in my teenage years. I wanted a pair of the latest and greatest skates, a pair of 595 Rydells' with a laser plate. I really wanted them badly. They had a program where you could earn Roller Bucks' In order to buy those skates, I remember, you had to have an amount that seemed almost impossible. With a lot of effort and perseverance, I did finally earn my skates, and I still have them to this day. They are one of my most prized possessions.

I learned of infatuation, heartbreak, friendships, and having relationships while at the rink. Skating gave me a sense of freedom in a world I felt so trapped in. It was my refuge and escape. I still treasure the memories of those days gone by. It was then I had my first REAL boyfriend. Yes, I "dated" guys at the skating rink, meaning I could couple skate and talk to them on the phone, but that was the extent of it.

I remember walking out of the skating rink one night,

and there were a group of guys hanging out by a car. They were telling me to come over to talk to them. I said no. They were like, "are you too good for us?" I had to laugh because I never wanted anyone to feel like I thought I was better than anyone. My life was a mess. So I walked over. That was my first mistake. Girls with low self-esteem are easy to get because there are looking for charming men who will say whatever they can to make them feel good. Girls, don't be deceived. You are better than that.

I met several of the guys, but one in particular stood out. He and I started talking. He looked like a rebel. He had long hair and seemed to be the leader of the pack. He was soft-spoken, whereas the other guys were yelling at all the girls and acting like fools. I had to leave, but he asked for my number. I was too embarrassed to tell him I was not allowed to go on a car date. That was something he later figured out. I was 15 when we met and turned 16 not too long after when I could officially go out. It was going to be a bit tricky.

I had gotten to know him over the phone and while hanging out with my girlfriends. He was known to get into fights and was the local bad boy. However, I saw a different person. Someone misunderstood and not catching

Chapter 4

a break. I had him meet my parents, but that didn't go so well. His long hair, muscle car, and bright red Reeboks didn't make the impression I was looking for. At the age of 16 and toward the end of 11th grade, this became an eventful year. I started trying drugs as an escape and fell head-over-heels in what I thought was love. I began to make even more of a train wreck out of my life. I thought I was doing great things. I was even feeling better about myself at times. However, I felt like I mattered because I "thought" someone truly loved me for once. My undeveloped brain wondered why this older guy would waste his time waiting on me. You believe you must be different, special and unique.

I wanted to be loved at all costs, to be needed and to be protected. It was the only thing that helped me. Having this guy as my boyfriend made my brothers stop beating me up. Yes, we grew up always fighting like cats and dogs. That was normal and just the way it was. We didn't just hit, we would throw whatever was around us. My oldest brother threw a knife one time. To this day, I'm thankful I wasn't in its path. Scott and Mark were fighting one day, and Mark ended up putting Scott's butt through the wall. They were destructive fights. I did my share of instigating. I finally had a boyfriend who would kick their butt, so the fighting

STOPPED. I felt empowered in so many ways. This was certainly the wrong type of empowerment. What did I know at the time? My brothers and I didn't know any different. Constantly hearing the fighting and acting it out was normal.

I realize the choices I made were what I needed at the time although not always best for me in the long run. I wouldn't have changed a thing in my situation during that time. Lord knows he protected me from many mishaps and was my saving grace in times of need. That year was a battle for me. My parents wanted to send my boyfriend to jail for statutory rape. He was 19. I was 16. The drama ensued for months, and we decided to go our separate ways when I graduated high school at 17. I realized I needed positive influences. I was extremely hurt and disappointed. I went through the stint of substance abuse with him and sometimes without him. I was never an abuser of drugs, but I was curious about EVERYTHING! I thought trying drugs would take me out of the reality I no longer wanted to be in. Only to find out, the feeling is temporary and the affects could be detrimental. I had to choose my path.

Ask Yourself:

Can you think back to what you did that made an

Chapter 4

impact on your belief system? Have you ever let someone else down? Have you had your hopes lifted only to be discouraged, AGAIN? What does love look like to you? Have you made some bad choices you later regretted? Do you wish you could turn back the hands of time? Do you wish you could have saved yourself for the right somebody? Are you searching for love in all the wrong places? Have you tried drugs and feel you can't stop now?

Life's Lessons:

The words you say and what you do for others can impact them for the rest of their lives. Are we being a positive role model or negative naysayer? Who you are and what you do will leave a lasting impression. Make sure it's one you'll be proud of.

Don't judge people. You never know someone's story. Be quick to understand when someone is acting out and encourage him or her to open up. You can't turn back the hands of time, but you can change starting today. There is a world waiting for you. Your story may give hope to others.

It doesn't matter what clothes you wear, where you come from, or how well you do. You can NEVER please everyone. Don't even try. I started seeing success and I was going places, but to others it seemed as if I was conceited and stuck-up. I wanted to be the one to fit in the right crowds and go to the finer places. Unfortunately, I didn't conform to what NORMAL was around there. Today, I'm grateful for not settling for mediocrity.

Chapter 5

(Establishing a New Flight Pattern)
Starting Over and Living on MY Terms

I WAS NOW 17 AND HAD GRADUATED FROM HIGH SCHOOL. I decided to move 3 ½ hours away to Richmond, VA. This was truly what I thought was the most difficult year of my life entering adulthood. I had counted the days until I could finally move out on my own, but that also meant I had to support myself. I moved in with a girl from my hometown that I really didn't know. We worked together at a local retail store. I thought she was pretty cool. I just really wanted to "GET OUT." I almost made the mistake of marrying the boyfriend to GET OUT, but realized being in that town would make my life miserable. I would have done exactly what my mom did, just to GET OUT! However, I didn't know it at the time, and today that boyfriend still lives with his dad, doesn't have a job anymore and was told by his father he wasn't well. Thank God for unanswered prayers. However, I wish him well. He's fighting a battle we don't know even know about.

We have all had roommate problems in the past, but I didn't see these problems coming. My roommate Dawn was going to college at VCU. I started a sales job for Thalhiemer's. I was fortunate enough to have a car while she had to ride the bus for transportation. My family helped me move out and get a fresh start. It was exhilarating. I saw the light at the end of the tunnel. This was it!

The first few weeks were AWESOME! FREEDOM, no parents, my own place, and I could stay out late if I want to. Then the partying began. We'd go to the clubhouse, meet up with new friends, and have a beer in the hot tub. I had a dose of reality, having to get up and go to work early every morning to pay the bills. I was BROKE. In a short three months with Dawn, we had gotten into our first fight. She was drinking at a party and came to wake me up because a guy had hit her. I tried to leave my tomboy days behind, but I put on a rough exterior to protect myself. However, when I went marching to the apartment where all the commotion was, I found out that she had poured beer in the guy's nose while he was sleeping. It was an automatic reaction for him to start swinging.

I went to help her out. I was in my pajamas, needed to go to work early in the morning, and people were partying everywhere. When I found out the truth, she then turned on me. I was stunned. I knew she was drunk, but she jumped

Chapter 5

on my back. I rolled her on the ground and told her to get up and go to bed. I went back to the apartment, and to my surprise, a guy I knew and his friend drove about 2 hours to say hello. I still kind of shake my head at that. It was a Saturday night, and he never called to tell me he was coming, but I was glad to see him given the situation.

Dawn and her friend came into the apartment. Out of nowhere, she throws my lamp and it breaks against the wall. My friend said, "Let's go for a ride." I hated the fact that I had to be at work so early, but the situation was not getting better, so we left. As we we're out on this ride, we see a guy stealing someone's bicycle and running with it. People were chasing him across the street. My thoughts were: what's happening here? They later dropped me off with my friend Rex, who lived in the complex nearby. Then they headed back home. Rex was the only person I knew from Richmond. The only problem was that it was my roommate's ex-boyfriend. BIG PROBLEM!

It seemed like a herd showed up at his door, banging and yelling. He let me stay the night to let them sleep it off. I went back to my apartment the next morning, and all of my clothes were on the lawn. Devastated, I picked up my clothes and threw them into my room. I got ready for work

Life in the Jetstream

as fast as I could. Later, my roommate apologized after the local resident assistant stepped in. Of course, it remained eventful in the next few months. I can probably write a separate book about all the events that happened during this one year. However, I'll save that for another time. This was the straw that broke the camel's back.

My roommate and her friends were partying at our complex, which was called Treehouse. It was an extension of VCU housing. I was low on gas and was waiting to get paid again because I had just paid rent. I was only 17 and couldn't put my name on the lease so I had to pay cash. We agreed to a certain date and I would put the money in MY cabinet. Many of you that have had roommates understand this term: my cabinet, with my food, and my stuff in the refrigerator. I decided to take the bus to the VCU campus to see a friend that night. I hadn't planned on staying very long. I just wanted something to do without spending any money.

Later that night, I saw Dawn and all of her friends at a FRAT party downtown. I asked her how she got to the party. She proceeded to tell me she drove my car until it ran out of gas, left it on the side of the road, and then caught a ride to the party. I was furious. I had to be at work the

Chapter 5

following morning and the bus was no longer running. I had to find us a way home. Our apartment was about 25 minutes away. There was one guy, who was willing to take us, but I was the only sober one and I worried if it was a good idea.

I didn't have any other options, and I agreed to let him take us back to our apartment. It was a kind gesture and desperately needed. I was attempting to be careful with the position I was putting us in. The minute we pulled into our complex in front of our apartment, I saw that our sliding door curtains were partly open and two men were inside. I knew they would run in the opposite direction thinking we would come in the normal way, so I ran in the other direction. There was one guy acting like he was hanging out on the balcony. I ran into the apartment and grabbed a long knife and went back outside. There was not a soul in sight at this point.

I headed back into the apartment, we called the police and I noticed ALL of my rent money was gone and some of MY food. We called the police and gave them our statements. During the investigation they found some of my food in the garbage. I was still too frantic to realize we had been robbed. It is such an invasion of privacy and trust. I was so upset that the car had to be dealt with the next day, and I had to skip a day of work. I slept on the floor in Dawn's room for the next couple of nights, fearful THEY would return. It is such a violation to know someone has ROBBED you! The detective was coming around asking questions again. Dawn started asking me for the rent money. I wasn't supposed to be living there because I was underage. This really put me in a bad spot. I didn't have any more money and didn't know where I was going to get it. What a feeling of hopelessness.

The detective solved the crime within a few days. The criminals lived upstairs from us. Dawn had met them on the bus from VCU where they were going to school for Criminal Justice. Can you believe that? I was shocked and appalled. Dawn did not want to press charges. I was offended, because it was my money that was stolen and she didn't want to press charges. I only wanted them to give the rent money back. She had left our door open and invited them to come down to join the party earlier. The detective encouraged me to move out, and without much hesitation, I did. I moved into a home with the detective's girlfriend and paid the same rent. It was on the opposite side of town, but without any drama.

Chapter 5

I continued to stay in Richmond. I had moved to a different area, so I looked for a job closer to where I was staying. I had always loved the airlines and thought I would try my luck at Richmond Airport. I was hired right away with Globe Security, which is now TSA. I was very excited about that job initially, and I learned quite a bit. I also lived a little through each passenger who shared his or her stories of travel. It was the ultimate dream to live a life jet-setting around the world. This job was easy, but learning to deal with co-workers was to become the challenge.

This job would prove to have long hours, very few breaks, and co-workers that walked all over me. Why? I didn't know how to stand up for myself, and when I did, the consequences I faced didn't seem worth it. My co-workers and manager would take two and three-hour lunch breaks to go shopping, they had several smoke breaks and it was all I could do to shove a sandwich down for lunch and take a bathroom break. I decided I would say something about the unfairness and blatant abuse of power. Of course, I would have let it go if I was only able to have my regular lunch time and go to the restroom when I needed to.

After the manager and co-workers came back from their

lunch shopping spree, I asked to talk to the manager in private. There was not really a place to go, but we stepped to the side and I began to politely let her know that what had been going on needed to be corrected. I wasn't prepared for what was to come. The manager began to share, with both her friend and my co-worker who I didn't approve of, what they were doing. What did she think about that?

Long story short, my manager proceeded to start yelling at me and chased me in the airport. A passenger came to my rescue. My manager, went after the passenger with her shoe as well. Needless to say, there was an investigation. I no longer wanted to work there, feeling like I would still be pushed around by the other co-workers who had stayed. The manager was fired and I walked away with another lesson learned. Don't wait to stand up for what's right. You will have less heartache and feel more confident. People will push you to see how far you will let them go. You have to establish boundaries. I didn't know how to do that during this time.

I had continued to work my other jobs while going to school. Once again I had to move because the girlfriend sold her home, which left me hanging. Was this a sign to

Chapter 5

leave Richmond? I couldn't imagine going back home. I would take my licks, however they came. I later quit the sales job at Thalhiemer's because they wouldn't let me off for Christmas to go home. I was very lonely, depressed, struggling to eat and make a life for myself. I didn't know trying to make a living would be so hard. I had been through a lot of challenges already in less than a year. I was not ready to move back, but I wanted to be in a familiar place. I'm sure you can relate from some point in your life.

I also worked for East Coast Entertainment. It was a great learning about the entertainment industry. I was a receptionist. Not so glamorous, but it came with a few perks. I got to know many of the band members and go to the venues. I understood the contracts and learned about riders. A rider on a contract for an artist lists the expectations that needs to be fulfilled, such as their equipment, transportation, and catering needs.

I also met people from Cellar Door, who were promoters for bigger events. I really enjoyed going to the shows and the vibe that always came with it. TGIF (Thank God It's Friday) was big in Richmond. I tried to go when it was feasible. I watched East Coast Entertainment in its infancy grow to the largest Entertainment Company on the

East Coast today. I thought one day I'd love to become an agent. However, I could not see myself in an office day after day. I knew that I didn't want to be in an office all the time, so I decided to interview for the FBI. I thought it would be more than pushing papers, and it was an alluring job that my Nana said would be beneficial for me. It was security and great money, she believed, so I decided to give it a shot.

I dressed up and headed to my interview. I was thrilled. We grow up wanting to be SOMEBODY! This job would solidify that. The first interview was amazing and seemed like things were going my way. They brought me back for a second interview where I met with a group this time. I believe they selected three other new hires. They laid a lot of rules and regulations on the table. It was as if we are in an interrogation room. They said, "You will have to take a lie detector test, you can have never taken drugs," and after that statement I couldn't hear another word. I was shocked and fearful that I'd be found out. Instead of talking to someone about what I had done, I chose not to go back the third time for the hiring process. I couldn't possibly be what they wanted, and I gave up. In hind-sight, they were probably waiting to see if I would just be honest.

Chapter 5

I continued working at a skating rink by night or whenever I could fill in. Being a competitive speed skater before, I still enjoyed coming to the rink. The 80's were big for the roller skating rink. Those were the days of having my first crushes, and trying to find out more about me. It was very helpful for me to be able to work all positions such as the DJ booth, snack bar, floor guard, skate shop, and ticketing. In Richmond, I would grab a bite to eat at the rink, nachos or hot dogs, when I went to work. It saved me many times because I was stressed to pay my bills and keep up. My new apartment complex I moved into gave me a ticket because they said my car was an eye sore. Really!

I remember briefly modeling in a BIG show for thousands of people in Richmond. I was also the stand-in model where I filled in for Miss Virginia, Dana Bryant on certain nights she couldn't be there. It was a moment in time to be remembered. The buzz was Billy Graham was in the audience with his daughter getting ready for her wedding. It was a dream-come true for me.

There was a period when living in Richmond that I was introduced to another world. Believe it or not, there is a fine line to cross when you've had some tiny success but are extremely broke. I had more psychological problems than I cared to admit. I can cover sexual abuse, daddy-love-me issues, low self-esteem, a mere child living on my own, and never felt protected or respected. I was in pure survival mode learning how to go it alone in a world that has plenty of sticks and stones to throw at you every chance it gets.

Following that, I was wondering how I was going to eat for the next week. I never wanted anyone to know how bad my situation was. I had confided in an older woman who I had befriended. She had seemed to be doing well. I didn't know exactly WHAT she was doing but she understood the problems I was having. There wasn't enough time in the day to have ANOTHER job. She asked me to talk to a guy that she was working with. I was invited to an upscale nightclub to take a look. They made it sound inviting. Good money and just a date for guys coming to town or for parties. Rules included a limit of two drinks, no personal information was to be exchanged, and they had to be discreet. Dress to impress.

I never knew at that point that she was an ESCORT, call girl, or whatever you wanted to call it. Is there a name to call a high-class prostitute? This goes without judgment because anyone can fall prey to the scam. This is also how girls sometimes get sold into slave trade. They tell you they

Chapter 5

have a modeling job for you in another city. You arrive at their mercy, needing the job and a place to stay venerable and alone. Ladies, please hear me. All legitimate job offers will have a contract and you will be able to verify it's a REAL company. Do your homework. Do yourself a favor, stay away from anything that feels uncomfortable? We see the red flags, we just don't listen.

I finally asked her if she had sex with the guys. She was evasive and said that she was "nice" to them. I read between the lines. I'm so thankful she used the word "nice" because that triggered the red flag for me. It reminded me of an old country song by Reba McEntire called "Fancy." The mom told the daughter, Fancy, to be nice to the gentleman and they'll be nice to you. I love the song because she left, took the high road and got the Georgia mansion in the end anyway.

I thank God that even though I was in a brutally low place, I couldn't bring myself to do that. I certainly don't judge women who become strippers, call girls, or drug addicts for that matter. In most cases, they have unresolved issues in their life and have chosen the path of a victim. It's easy! Sometimes they can't see past the last drink or trick. When you are so far down you need help getting up. It's

71

difficult to value yourself when you have never established what that means to you. Think about this, just because you are not getting "paid" for a job like this, every relationship you have, you are giving a piece of yourself away for FREE! We need to value ourselves, our minds and our bodies.

In my situation, I was a young, blonde woman trying to find my way at 17 all alone. That's what most would see as being vulnerable and falling into the traps or webs of life. I could have been one of them. Fortunately, I had a taste of a better future. I had someone who inspired me and that I didn't want to let down. You may not have that someone in your family or circle of friends right now and its okay. Find a support team that works for you. If you do have someone to talk to, communicate how you feel and tell them what's on your mind. I feared rejection or getting laughed at. I was ashamed of some of my actions. My reasoning had not always been on track although I tried my best.

My mom had called me and asked if I would do ONE last pageant. With some consideration I agreed. When I was 15 and 16 years old, I had done so many pageants that I no longer wanted to do them anymore. I felt I learned what I needed. Now, I was going to represent Virginia in

Chapter 5

Hawaii at the Young Miss of America pageant. Who would say NO to Hawaii? That had been a DREAM of mine. The competition was based on interview, state costume, swimsuit, and evening gown. It was also a scholarship pageant so I had to be in college and maintain a 3.5 GPA. I loved visiting Hawaii for the first time. I was in awe of the beautiful waters, the tours of the island, the international marketplace, and the luau was surreal. Going to Hawaii was a break I needed. Meeting other girls and being on an exotic island that most only dream of going to open the door for me to broaden my horizons.

I didn't see it coming, but it was definitely to my amazement. I WON the pageant! I know what you're thinking: what do you mean you WON? I won the National pageant representing Virginia. Girls had come from all over and they chose me. This became another essential time in my life. My world was never the same after that experience. I was whisked off to sign contracts, understand the rules, and began the next morning with breakfast as the reigning Young Miss of America. People were coming to the table asking for my autograph and all of the state winners were more than gracious. I went to take a swim that day. I believe it was the only time I didn't wear my crown and banner. I remember coming back to my room and the maid was trying on my crown. First, I was upset thinking she'd break it, but I quickly shifted my attitude. It was adorable. We all dream about that special moment. We believe in the possibilities of a better tomorrow. That brief moment in time she was a beauty queen. I think all women need to experience what it means to be "Queen for a Day!"

My dreams had started coming true. The doors had begun flying open for me. It was hard work making it to all of the appearances. I traveled all over the U.S. and met many different people. I was fortunate enough to do so many things. However, in order to maintain my 3.5 GPA for the scholarship and travel to 75% of all state pageants, I could not maintain my living arrangements and multiple jobs at 18. Something needed to change.

My mom and dad asked me to move back in with them. I could work and go to school and it freed my time to travel as well. Extremely reluctant, I agreed. I knew I could not do this any other way. When I decided to do the pageant, it was meant as an escape. I was thrilled with what was to come, but I wanted to do it on my own. I had started a job at Wal-Mart and also worked for my best-friend, Jen's dad at a collection agency. I also enrolled in the local community college to keep up my GPA.

Chapter 5

I started flying out most weekends for appearances. I would teach the dances for the opening number for many of the state pageants, sing from time to time, and emcee. I had to travel in crown and banner to and from the events. I was treated like royalty. I did get a little taste of celebrity. Everyone wanted to talk to me, get photographs and autographs. I loved it in the beginning until I started having nightmares in my hotel room in Sacramento, CA. I dreamt that people were looking through my hotel window staring at me. I felt they were knocking on my door, and I was a bit paranoid at times. I felt I could not be the perfect role model that people were looking for. I felt the standards were too high to live up to. Living under the microscope is NOT what anyone wants. I was hiding under the mask that I was going to be found out, thinking: I'm not the good girl they think I am. I began to empathize with celebrities and their loss of privacy. I know I didn't touch the surface compared to what most celebrities face daily.

My journey of events began with me riding an elephant for Ringling Bros. Barnum and Bailey Circus. I was fortunate enough to see Oprah, Phil Donahue, and Geraldo on my tour through New York. I was interviewed by Regis, on the Regis and Kathie Lee talk show when Sammy Davis Jr. and Barbara Walters were there. I shared the Silver

Screen with major icons. Later, I received a letter from Oprah that I've kept to this day. Her words of wisdom were: "Do what you are passionate about and success will follow." I had always admired Oprah. Oprah's talk show changed the way we see and think. She talked about her abuse openly and allowed others not to feel isolated. During my trip in New York I met Ron Palin, the look-alike for Gorbachev. I enjoyed my first trip to Las Vegas. The lights were mesmerizing. I was grateful to have the National Teen winner, Natasha, with me during part of the tour.

My most exciting trip was to Los Angeles. My childhood dream was to go to Hollywood. I was going to be in a sitcom with some of the oldest and renowned stars at Sunset Gower Studios. Wow! I was a girl from the other side of the tracks making her debut on the Silver Screen. What were the chances? I was only on set for a few days. I even had a few lines, but the experience was unbelievable.

I had my own dressing room, wardrobe, make-up, and met some extraordinary people. I even wore one of Cher's dresses. I didn't want to miss any of the action going on the stage while I was there. After I was dressed, I sat in the stands to watch the process. However, I got booted back to

Chapter 5

my dressing room for the first few scenes because my beaded dress made too much noise when I moved.

I met Pat Priest Hansing, who played Marilyn Munster from the Munster's Show. She was still beautiful and had a heart of gold. I was playing myself, Toni Thomas, Young Miss of America. I was working directly with Norm Crosby. I didn't know who he was at the time. He was funny and extremely hospitable to me. I remember on the second day of filming he was so excited. He couldn't wait for me to meet his good friend, Ernie, who turned out to be Ernest Borgnine. I did recognize Norm Fell, who played Mr. Roper on Three's Company. I became friendly with Allen Garfield, even flying his dog from LA to New York at one point. Pat Priest Hansing had set her son, Lance and I, up on a date later before I decided to move to LA. We had dinner and he showed me around town. Steve Levitt was also on set. It was great watching the dynamics. My first experience on set was a magical one.

During the first day of filming I had a lunch date with Gary Goch. I had met him previously through another pageant director when I had won the Miss Roanoke Teenager pageant. He was a judge. Gary had produced several movies. The most memorable was A Christmas

Story in the 1950's. He would send me scripts and talked often about me being a Queen and having my ladies in waiting. He happened to be in LA while filming, even though he lived in New York. We had a nice lunch and talked about what I was doing on tour. It was a treat. He loved my excitement and enthusiasm. That was something most of them don't see after being in the industry for so many years.

It was Mother's Day weekend when, during lunch, I went next door to the local drugstore. I was looking for something to give my mother since I would be arriving home on Mother's Day. I bought a grey sweatshirt at the store across from the studio. I couldn't be with my mom, but wanted to do something memorable for her. She lived her life through what I did and this was a way to say thank you without words. I decided to have the cast from the HBO sitcom "Some Like It Hot" autograph the sweatshirt. They all wrote "Happy Mom's Day" or "to Toni's mom" They were incredible. I still have the sweatshirt and will treasure the fond memory of that weekend. It stands for the DREAM both my mom and I pursued.

Soon after I returned home, my brother brought a friend home from Fort Bragg. They were both serving in the

Army. This guy had graduated from the same high school as we did, just four years earlier. I had always thought he was handsome. We met that night, talked and danced at the party. That night was the first of several years to come. We started dating. He would stay late at my house, driving back without sleep to Fort Bragg before sunrise for PT (physical training). His life had been tragic after 1981; I knew he was a fighter and a survivor. I mean, physically, he wouldn't take anything from anybody. His brother was shot and killed, his mother committed suicide, and his best friend fell off a building one night and died when they were partying. I thought I would be the one to HELP SAVE him. Boy, I didn't know what was in store for me. I also didn't know how closely our lives would mirror one another.

I continued to travel and make appearances. When summer came, the pageant director wanted me to go on the road for a two-month, non-stop tour. Wal-Mart was terrific because they allowed me to take off whenever I needed. I learned how to work in most positions throughout the store. They could use me wherever they needed when I was back in town. I also made an appearance for the ribbon cutting of the Grand Opening of the store that I was employed at.

I was overjoyed to get started on the tour. The

weekends I would fly in and out were like a teaser. After the first few weeks on tour I started getting tired. We were in the van often, going from hotel to hotel, setting up at each state pageant and breaking down. My calls would get monitored because of the standard that had to be upheld for the rules and regulations. We had adjoining rooms, so basically no privacy. I was going to bed late and getting up super early. I often cried myself to sleep many nights. I felt sorry for Miss USA's and Miss America's with the grueling schedules they endured in comparison. I felt like a puppet and people couldn't truly know me.

The relationship between the director and me was starting to get strained during that tour. Communication started breaking down and I asked my mom to come pick me up in Atlanta. I didn't want to be on the road anymore. I only had a few more shows to do, but I needed to leave. I had more than met my responsibility as the reigning titleholder. After returning home, the pageant director called and told my mother that they would no longer pay for her to come back with me to Hawaii to pass on my crown. Then things started getting unpleasant. It was stated in my contract when I won that my mom would be able to travel with me. I had a chaperone just about every step of the way. So what had changed?

Chapter 5

I ended my reign in Hawaii and even though stressful in the end, the experience changed my thought process forever. From this point on, I knew I could do or meet anyone I wanted to. I WAS worth it. I can't say I believed it fully since my self-esteem was so low for so many years. I still needed validation and acceptance to feel worthy. You've heard the old saying, "Shoot for the moon, the worst thing that can happen is you land among the stars." That's exactly what I was going to do. I had a BIGGER DREAM. That's not to say I did not fight with myself daily. I still had the chatterbox telling me that I wasn't good enough: Quit being silly, these DREAMS aren't for YOU! You're a joke. Wait till they really know who you are and what you've done.

Ask Yourself:

Have you ever made hasty decisions in your life? Have all of your jobs been smooth transitions? Have you had "LUCKY" breaks? Have you had the chatterbox (self-talk) talk you into or out of situations? Have you had that person or persons in your life that you wanted to "SAVE?" Have you wished for something so badly then got it and regretted it? What opportunities have you been given and didn't take advantage of?

Life's Lessons:

Don't move in with people you don't know. Set boundaries early in your relationships. I know we are not supposed to trust strangers, but some people are put in our paths as ANGELS to guide us. Remember strangers will eventually become your spouse, co-worker, friend, or business partner. Sometimes in life we WISH for many things. We never know what the repercussions will be. We also need to take personal responsibility for our actions.

I'm thankful for the good and the bad, because it makes us be more specific when we are asking for something in the future. Be careful what you WISH for; it might come TRUE! Sometimes we NEED to save ourselves before we ever think we can help another. I love the quote, "Luck is when preparation meets opportunity" Seneca. Opportunities are everywhere if you just open your eyes. You need to be open to receive them.

Chapter 6

(Taking a Nosedive)
Recognizing Conflict When it Happens

I WENT BACK TO WORKING AT WAL-MART AND LIVING IN MY SMALL TOWN following the tour. When I returned to Hawaii to pass on my title, I had met someone there who wanted me to do some modeling for his company. Unfortunately, the director said no, but I met with him to see his clothing line. It was the hottest fashion those days. All of the state winners had bought them. The drop seat pants with the crop tops. This became my first business, Fantasia Enterprises. I continued to work at Wal-Mart and hired friends to work for me at the mall. I purchased a kiosk and started importing the outfits.

I also put the clothes in tanning salons, generating income that way as well. Interesting enough, I learned some tough business lessons during this time. It was expensive owning and setting up my business. I had to carry a large insurance policy in case someone got hurt. Workers wouldn't show up on time or would leave early. On weekends, they would pay themselves cash out of the till. I think what hurt me the most was learning how people get their information. An older gentleman I was selling to at one tanning salon seemed so sweet. He asked me a million questions, all of which I politely answered. Basically, what he was doing was finding out who I bought from and went directly to the source to completely cut me out. That was a hard lesson for me to learn. You sometimes have to guard certain information. Some people may want more than you're willing to give.

I started spending more time with my boyfriend now that my world was a bit quieter after my pageant year. We had a lot of fun and did everything together. As time went on, he began to party more often. I didn't mind it every now and then, but I didn't want my life to go in that direction. I knew he used alcoholism as a way of escape, but my mind took me back to being a child of other alcoholics. That path only leads to destruction. We broke up for a brief period of time.

After coming back from LA working on the sitcom, I earned enough money to buy my dream horse. I bought a jet-black Arabian gelding. It was another dream fulfilled. One day, I had been out at the barn grooming my horse. On my way home, someone ran a red light and crashed into me on the driver side. I was slumped partly in the passenger

Chapter 6

seat. A crowd gathered and I could hear some background noise, but couldn't respond or open my eyes. I was transported to the hospital by ambulance.

Luckily, I only had a concussion and minor injuries. My second night at home I guess my ex- boyfriend found out about the accident and he drove 3 hours to come see me. He snuck into my family's home and left love notes for me all over my bedroom, in the closet, pillow cases, and my shoes. He didn't know I was sleeping in my brother's old room next to mine. He could have been shot because my dad kept a gun beside his bed. As nice as it was at the time, you don't come into people's homes in the middle of the night. That was his way of showing me he cared. He never knew how to show love and I never knew how to receive it. That was such a heartfelt gesture for him

We talked on the phone often. He started coming to see me again and got back together. Well, one night I was working till about 10 p.m. I was going to set one of Ricky's friends up with my co-worker on a double date. I stopped by the friend's house and set up the date. I arrived at home about 11:30 p.m. It was a Friday night. I walked in the door and my dad tells me to follow him back to my car. It had just been fixed from the accident only weeks before. He begins to take his fist and started punching holes in the windshield. His hand was bloody and I was standing there thinking: what did I do? A million things were going through my head. I had lived on my own, traveled, met awesome people and WHY was this happening to me? The chaos never seemed to go away. I was a magnet to it for some reason. I wondered what will my life look like down the road: will it get easier?

My mom had to drive me to work the next day so he could get my car fixed again that week. Once it was fixed, I asked Ricky's dad if I could move in with him. Ricky lived at Fort Bragg most of the time. His dad agreed. Although I really didn't want to make this transition, I felt I had nowhere else to go. I needed enough time to think about where I wanted to move or what I wanted to do. I didn't want to stay in that town any longer. I felt the town and people wanted to see me fail. I kept getting beat down so I didn't want to look back with regrets. I wanted a fresh start to reevaluate my life.

I was happy about the move and felt a sense of relief. Ricky and I were working things out. Even though he continued to drink heavily, I still stayed. I felt it was a better alternative for me. A few months went by and Ricky

Chapter 6

asked if I would come see him in Fort Bragg. I met him at a hotel. Most of the time, I went to Fort Bragg, we would stay at my brother's place off base. Ricky lived on base. He wanted to stay at a hotel. We hadn't been there an hour before he wanted to show me his NEW toy. It was a 10MM gun. He had not yet registered. I stood up and took a look. I didn't like guns very much anyway. He showed me the safety was on and did not put his finger near the trigger. I had decided to sit back on the bed and watch TV when the next thing I knew, the gun went off.

I had been shot! I jumped out of bed and I grabbed my arm. His eyes were so big and he turned white. He ran to me and wanted to see. I didn't want to let go of my arm. I showed him where I was shot and he took a towel and wrapped a tourniquet around my arm. It was an incident you cannot possibly believe is happening to you in the moment. I was in shock. He grabbed my keys to take me to the hospital. I had a brand new car he hadn't seen yet. I had just bought this car and was very particular about it. As he drove me to the hospital he began to smoke in my new car. I was crying and telling him not to smoke in the car. He said he had to and that he was sorry. He was telling me what we should say so he wouldn't get kicked out of the military. I don't recall much other than obviously on one particular road in Fort Bragg they have a lot of drive by shootings. He told them I just arrived in town, which was true, and we had stopped to get something from the trunk of my car.

We arrived at the hospital, he told me to wait in the car for a minute. I saw him go up the hill into the woods beside the hospital and hide the gun. It wasn't registered. He knew he'd be in a lot of trouble. Luckily, the hole in my arm was a ricochet from the gun and the shavings. It caused a large hole in my left arm. It was a blessing in disguise, because another two centimeters the bullet would have killed me. The shavings caused enough damage in my arm, and it was extremely painful. They cleaned my wound, bandaged it, and put a sling on my arm.

I was then released from the hospital. We went back to the hotel and checked out immediately. There were no police there or phone messages of any kind. There wasn't any indication that anyone called about a gunshot. He was paranoid and wanted to go somewhere else. I only chose to leave that room because you could see the hole from the gunshot in the bed. The next problem would be explaining to my parents what had happened to me. I had a few days left to figure it out. It was odd, but Ricky wanted us to go

Chapter 6

see Born on the 4th of July with Tom Cruise. He was so apologetic. I could tell he was speechless. Tragedy had always seemed to follow him. This was no different.

I went back home and couldn't tell the truth about what really happened. My arm was wrapped and I had a sling on. I knew my dad didn't believe my story. I was a bad liar. I'm a deer in the headlights when telling a story that deviates from the truth. I didn't want them hating him for being so irresponsible. We continued to date for months after that. Ricky decided without asking me, that he would get out of the Army to spend more time with me. He had a rough bout at Ranger school in the survivor program so he came home for good. It was fine in the beginning, but the partying became more than I could stand. I began looking for a WAY OUT! I didn't know how to tell him I didn't want to date anymore. I couldn't handle the partying. He thought we'd live happily ever after. Truthfully, I don't think either of us believed in fairytales.

I enjoyed the traveling so much while on tour with the pageant system that I kept asking myself how I could fly without having to pay for it. There was a girl from my high school that had been hired with a major air carrier. She told me to go to an open house. I found the first one and went

Life in the Jetstream

immediately. This was my WAY OUT! I didn't tell Ricky until I got the call back from the company to come to Chicago and do the second interview. I received a letter to come for the physical. This was all going so fast. The company sent me a lot of paperwork to fill it out and use as a study guide for training. They told me they would have a training date soon. I was ecstatic. I was going to be a FLIGHT ATTENDANT. A world traveler!

I continued to stay at Ricky's and his dads even as they made the move about half hour away. I was glad he was being supportive. He helped me study and learn military time. We'd go boating and skiing, and we began to have some fun again. However, my mind was made up. I got a training date and told Ricky I needed to start packing. They gave me two weeks. It was a week before I left and Ricky says to me, "You're not REALLY going ARE YOU?" I was dumbfounded. I thought to myself: what was all this work and practicing for? I told him I needed to do this for me. When I talked to Rick's dad years later, he said the moment I told him I was leaving to go to flight attendant training was the moment he knew our relationship was over. He told his dad, "I'll meet someone that can offer me the world. It's a lost cause." We did try to continue dating, but he was right in the end.

Ask Yourself:

What has someone done in your life that you still shake your head about today? Do you wonder HOW the chaos follows you? Do you hope that certain situations turn out in your favor? Why should I trust anyone? Why can't I find Mr. Right? Why do I attract the same type of men and same type of situations to my life? Am I worthy of more? Can I change my path? Does it get easier? Have you lied to protect others? Have you not had the words to speak when you need to make a change?

Life's Lessons:

You learn to reach a point in your life where you start asking yourself, "What am I supposed to learn from this?" In business, I learned that not everyone is going to have integrity, so use caution. I appreciated the fact that I could be given opportunities, but what I choose to do with them was up to me. Your circumstances will define you, only if you let them. Evaluate why people are in your life.

You will continue to attract the same type of people and situations until you change the pattern. You have to want to change. You are worth fighting for. Your path is paved by decisions you make. Nobody ever said life would be easy, you just have to make it worth it!

Life in the Jetstream

You will face opposition your entire life. The good news if you've already learned the lesson it does get easier. You are better equipped to handle it. Finding your voice and creating boundaries in your life will protect you in the future. Some of you may judge your character because of choices you made. Today is a new day, you can begin again. We all make mistakes.

Chapter 7

**(First Class Ticket to Paradise - or NOT!)
Living the Dream, or So I Thought**

I WENT TO FLIGHT ATTENDANT TRAINING AT 19 YEARS OLD. It was July 6, 1990. I was happy to be in Chicago, Illinois, training for my DREAM job. To my surprise, the first base I selected was Los Angeles. I couldn't wait for the adventure, bright lights, big stars, and red carpets. My mom drove my car out to Los Angeles; and she took my new roommates around until they found an affordable apartment. Unfortunately, I had to work during the first week. There were four of us in a two-bedroom apartment in Torrance, California. We were broker than broke. I was glad to have a place in Los Angeles; I just couldn't go too far. Every time I'd get a call from Ricky, my roommates would ask him who was calling and he would go NUTS! He wanted to know who else would be calling me.

The roommate situation later fizzled out very quickly. The girl I was sharing a room with, Tracie, was from Denver and kept a pet rat in our closet. She was a rocker chick from the word go. She wore three-inch stiletto heels, was a brunette and had long hair. She was a free spirit and that's why I liked her so much at first. I realized later that we didn't have that much in common. Within the first year she was separated from the company. Tina was a bubbly Asian girl. She laughed a lot. She continued to work on the West Coast. Kristen was from the East coast, very petite and mild-mannered. She was just a sweet person. Unfortunately, Kristin later passed away to cancer in her thirties. We all flew different schedules so never really had a chance to hang out and really get to know each other very well.

I ended up meeting my dad's brother, Gary, whom he was estranged for many years. He and his wife lived in Los Angeles. They were gracious enough to let me stay with them in Granada Hills for a few months. I got to know them, and they were an awesome couple. They would give me advice, and I am forever grateful for their help. I was only in LA a brief ten months before I decided to move to London, England. I didn't know how to say goodbye to Ricky, so distance was the answer for me. Once again I ran from my problems instead of facing them.

When I was offered the opportunity to go to London, I had no idea where it was. I didn't pay much attention to geography in school. My girlfriend Natasha, who was the

Chapter 7

Teen Young Miss of America winner who I previously toured with, lived in LA. She had a friend who lived in London and owned a bed and breakfast. I thought why not. I always wanted to travel around the world. I was afraid of being alone across the ocean, but I could do this!

The bed and breakfast was wonderful. It was three stories high with ten bedrooms, four bathrooms, a kitchen, and a sitting room where we'd go for high tea. High tea just means you'll have cookies and biscuits with tea at around 4 in the afternoon. There was an adorable garden that the owners took pride in showing to the guests. I was given instructions on how to escape the third floor in the event of fire, told how often my room would be cleaned, how to use the pay telephone, when breakfast would be served, and several other need-to-know items. I was experiencing a whole new world and I embraced it.

I moved over in March 1991. Everything in the sense that I knew was different. The British accents, public transportation, and rainy days were a culture shock. The architecture was amazing, the energy was phenomenal, but the cost of living was less than desirable. I had also NEVER bagged my own groceries and have to pay for them on top of that. I would visit the local KFC and have to

Life in the Jetstream

pay 10 pence per pack of ketchup. Just unbelievable! In America, we are used to everything being super-sized. Well, so much for that. It was a good thing for me to experience.

We had to register at the police station when we arrived within the first two weeks. There, I met Kerri, who has been one of my closest friends. She was a flight attendant and had moved over there as well from Northern California. We would venture out together, checking out the sights and sounds. We did love going to Hard Rock Café. They had the BEST hot fudge brownie sundaes. They were such a treat. Although she only stayed for nine months, we created a lifelong friendship. Kerri became one of my partners in crime throughout the next several years.

I was lying in bed at the B&B in Ealing Common. I saw an advertisement where WWF (World Wrestling Federation), now called WWE, was at the Royal Albert Hall that night. Well, I knew several of the guys from when I lived in Richmond. I saw that Ric Flair would be there so I jumped in my clothes and took the train to Royal Albert Hall. I had only been in London less than a month. I went to the back door and started knocking on it. There were two twin referees Dave & Earl who worked for WWF. Dave opened the door and said, "Toni what are YOU doing in

Chapter 7

London?"

I replied, "I live here now."

Dave said, "You have to come in. Ric would love to see you. He's wrestling right now, but he'll be off in a few minutes."

The wrestlers were lined up on the walls. Ric always treated me somewhat like a daughter if you want to call it that. I remember Ric said to me one time, "You don't need to be around all of this partying" I always had a great time, but he was right. I saw a lot of things that 17 or 18 year old shouldn't see. Ric was everything he said on TV. He was free-spirited, loved the limos, the ladies, fancy restaurants, and all the finer things in life. He dressed like a million bucks and had an amazing zest for life. I always appreciated the fact that he respected me. That industry didn't breed many gentlemen. He was also a player but treated me well.

As Ric came back from the ring, he was sweaty and out-of-breath. Dave caught him whispered in his ear, and pointed in my direction. Ric was surprised and immediately came over and gave me a hug. He said, "Don't go anywhere, we are going out tonight." Stringfellow's was the trendiest dance club in London at the time. It was where ALL the stars would go. After living in LA, I had been introduced to Peter Stringfellow and Roger, who were in charge of the Beverly Hills night club. Peter was considered to be the Hugh Hefner of England. I just thought he was a flamboyant man with his entourage of beautiful women. I had made my way to see Roger and reconnected when I arrived in London. This would be my second time seeing him within the month.

There were about 25 of us who went out that night. I danced with Gene Oakland, who was the ring announcer. Ric introduced me to some of the others. We had a blast laughing and joking. It was a hopping place. I met someone else that night from the Chippendale corporation. He invited me to come see their show the following week at The Strand Theatre. Hesitant, I thought it was the type of place where you stick dollars in the G-strings. I didn't like that kind of thing, but he said this was a REAL SHOW, a big production, we exchanged numbers. Ric had once again gained the attention of the entire club by being the life of the party. Some things never changed. It was a great night to take me away from my new-found existence and just let go, have a blast, and I did just that!

Chapter 7

The following week, the guy who I had met at the club had called. He told me to pick up my ticket at the will call booth. I asked if I would be seeing him at the show. He said it was a very busy time for him during the show, but he'd stop by to say hi. I was alone and felt awkward, but I was always adventurous enough to try new things. I saw an older couple there, and I thought that was peculiar. I decided to go over and start talking to them. They told me they were visiting their son, a dancer in the show. They came to celebrate his birthday.

I found out that the father was a pilot for another major airline so we had a few things in common. They lived in LA, where I had just moved from. They seemed like such a glamorous couple. They invited me to go to dinner with them at Hard Rock Café to celebrate Victor's birthday. I didn't know anyone in town so I decided to go. They said he'd be in town for a few months with the show. We had a great time that night, and Victor and I exchanged information.

Victor and I became good friends. Victor told me all the guys missed GNC the most from the states, so when I flew a trip to New York, I would pick up protein powder for them every now and then. I would mainly fly to New York because I wanted to see friends and venture out to experience new things. I arrived in New York one morning and decided to take a walk around the block. We were staying at the Milford Plaza. The crews called it the Mildew Plaza. No worries, it has been renovated since then. The best thing about that hotel was location, location, and location.

I started out on my walk around the block and was three quarters of the way back to my hotel. There was a man in a gray business suit with, clean-cut dark hair, jogging towards me. I was taken back and started walking faster. He caught up to me and started small talk. I was thinking: what the heck he is doing? He gave me his card. He was President of some type of modeling agency. I've seen this WAY too many times before with pageants and living in LA. He was also telling me his picture was on the front of The New York Times. He asked if I knew who he was. We have a funny joke with the airline when someone asks us, "Do you know who I am?" We want to pick up to PA and ask the other passengers if they know who the passenger is, because obviously he doesn't remember. He seemed proud of being on the cover of The New York Times.

He walked with me until I stopped in front of my hotel.

Chapter 7

At that point, the second London crew was getting out of the van. One of the girls said, "Hey Toni did you just get in today?"

I replied, "Yes." This was the ONLY information this guy had.

He told me to call him, and I said I would. It was amusing because he said, "I know you're NOT going to call." Now if he knew that, why would he still want to call me? It was unusual and uncomfortable to meet someone that just ran to catch me on the street, so I wasn't going to call.

I went into the hotel to take a nap. It was about 6 p.m. and my phone rings. It was the guy from earlier who had somehow found my room without having my last name or room number. I asked him WHY he was calling me and HOW he got my information. He said he thought I would be impressed that he had connections. I told him I was not. I had heard of many stories in THAT hotel where women were raped and murdered. I was only 20 years old. I spoke to him briefly and later went out with the crew for dinner.

I explained what happened earlier that morning. I mentioned what he said about being on the cover of The

Life in the Jetstream

New York Times.

One of the guys immediately said, Stay away from him and throw his card away," which is what I did. I flew back to London the following day. I had awoken to a phone call from New York. This guy had found me once again. Now, I was furious. I asked him why he was calling me and told him it's not appropriate to track women down. I was not impressed. He said he only wanted ONE date. That's it! After what I heard about this guy, I was afraid to say yes or no. He had found me twice and there was no hiding.

This guy was on the front page of The New York Times. He was in a conspiracy with George Steinbrenner owner of the Yankees to dig up dirt on Hall of Famer Dave Winfield. His name was Howard Spiro. I was told he was CONNECTED! I told him I was not comfortable with the whole thing. I didn't feel safe. He assured me, he'd explain everything at dinner. That is wasn't true what they were saying about him. I didn't have anything to worry about. I finally agreed to go on one date and I told him my "rules." He was nice enough to agree and tried to make me feel at ease. I didn't want any personal cars picking me up, or anyone coming to my hotel room. I would meet him in the lobby. I needed the name and address of where we were

Chapter 7

going, so we had scheduled the "date." My flight to New York was cancelled and when I got back to the B&B, I was going to give him a courtesy call. When I called to let him know my flight had cancelled, he already knew. Of course, he did.

Finally, the day had come and I landed in New York. Our dinner plans were set. I left all the information with my crew and called home to let mom know. As I was getting ready, the doorbell rang. I was startled because one of the rules was he couldn't come to my room. I looked out the door and two security guards were standing there, one with a bag in his hand. I asked what they wanted. One said, "We have a delivery from the gentleman downstairs." I opened the door and they gave me the bag. Inside was a box of Godiva chocolates with a note. It started off with "Dear Goddess" and finished with a poem. I thought to myself: what have I gotten myself in to? I met him downstairs, thanked him for the gift, and then he hailed a cab to his favorite Italian restaurant. We were going to Tavern on the Green, but it was under construction at the time.

It was like a scene from a movie. Everyone greeted us as we entered. He was a local celebrity. The maître d' said the best seat in the house was reserved for us this evening.

The owners were having dinner together, and Howard introduced me to his close friends. He was sharply dressed and looked like he walked out of GQ magazine. I had on a pink three-quarter-length dress. There were candles on the table and light music played in the background. He didn't drink, but asked if I'd like one. I needed one about then, so he ordered a red wine. OK, so I was under age, but it was so necessary at the time. He ordered dinner for us and it was wonderful.

He tried explaining what happened with George Steinbrenner and Dave Winfield. I could see him talking, but I couldn't tell you the first thing he said. The meal was over and the maître d' said he had something special for me. He brought out a big white box with balloons on it. Inside was a big, white, super-soft, Gund teddy bear. They were extremely popular at the time. It was a very expensive gesture and was making me feel even more awkward. As we were departing, I received roses as a send-off. There was no doubt he was charming, romantic, well-put-together, relatively handsome, and knew how to treat a lady.

Unfortunately, it was doomed from the beginning. The way we met on the streets, him finding me without my permission, and all the expensive gifts were not the way to

Chapter 7

MY heart. I have respect for him, because he did stay true to his word. Only one date, and if I wasn't interested, he wouldn't pursue me any further. I didn't hear back from him ever again.

I can't say my luck got any better after that. I did fly the trips to New York often when I started flying out of London. I wanted to see what the hype was all about. Within nine months that my girlfriend, Kerri, was leaving London soon, we decided to do a trip together. She had a friend in town that was going to show us around the city. We were excited about going out. She said her friend had a friend, and they were setting me up on a blind date. We were going to paint the town and we did. When someone says BLIND date, you are CONCERNED.

I was really along for the ride and was comforted that they were two of New York's finest. We'd be protected in the BIG APPLE. When I saw this guy, he was attractive. He looked like he just stepped out of Muscle & Fitness magazine. I was thrilled. They picked us up and we headed for a nightclub. I immediately started realizing that he had zero respect for women, was rude to others, and being conceited was a polite word to describe him. He became unbearable. I quit drinking after just two drinks because he was telling me to go get him drinks. I was exhausted, and I was so over this guy that I just wanted to leave. I thought: no big deal, I'm in New York. I can handle it for a few more hours.

Well, the night was ending and we were ready to go back to the Milford Plaza. Kerri's friend asked if they could walk us to the room. I was giving her the BIG EYEBALLS, saying NOOOOOOOOO. She said, "Please?" I said, "We are going to your room then." Her room was about four doors down from mine. When we got to her room, her friend asked if we could give them a few minutes alone. He asked if it would be okay. I cringed, and said, "okay" for the brief time. I opened my door and turned on the TV for us to watch. Here is a time I look back on and say, if only I would have done something different. It was a BIG RED FLAG!

He walked in my room, started taking off his clothes to jump in the shower. I said, "WHAT ARE YOU DOING?" I was in complete shock. I was paralyzed wondering what to do next.

He replied nonchalantly, "Taking a shower." I couldn't believe what was happening. I panicked and ran out of the

Chapter 7

room to a flying partner's room. His name is Daniel. Daniel was Kerri's roommate in London. He was a super-quiet, reserved Asian guy. I ran out of my room while this guy was in my shower and started banging on Daniel's door. It was 2:30 a.m. in the morning. I didn't know what to do.

My mind was racing. I told him in my rambling words, "There is a man that's naked in my hotel room that I don't want there to call security." I guess I was thinking security could get there right away and get him out while I waited in Daniel's room or should I go back to my room before they get there? I had left my purse and everything so I ran back to the room, and it dawns on me that he's a cop. How is this going to work? The plan slowly started deteriorating. It was too late for me to leave again because he was out of the shower, and here comes security knocking on my door. Two security officers were standing there. They were overweight guys who looked like they just woken up, and I knew I was doomed.

The security guards asked if I was okay, and I'm trying to give them the EYEBALL stare. I was thinking: why are you overreacting? He's an idiot, he'll be leaving soon. Just let it go. I just knew they could see I was scared. This guy then asks them what they are doing there as he proceeds to

107

tell them he is a COP! He was standing there in a towel as if it were his room. The door closes, they leave, and he asked whether I called security. I said "NO!" For many years, I blacked out what happened next.

He was angry that the security guards came to the room. He shoved me up against the door and tried to kiss me and I said "NO." He turned me toward the bed and pushed me down. I kept pushing him off saying "Stop it. As he started pulling at my clothes, he eventually held me down by sitting on top of me with one hand over my mouth and one hand holding both my hands above my head. He told me I better not scream, nobody would believe me anyway and I'll make it worse. When he removed his hand from my mouth, I couldn't scream even if I wanted to. I couldn't find my voice anywhere. I felt defeated. I didn't know what was going to be worse getting raped or beat. I had no idea what would happen, so I quit fighting with him and gave up.

My original memory of this event was being forced against the door, and later curled up in the fetal position on the bed, crying wondering WHY? I blamed myself, thinking I had asked for it. He acted as if he were entitled to do whatever he wanted. I remained quiet about it for years as I was embarrassed and ashamed. I didn't know how to

Chapter 7

speak up. Rape is a violent crime. Those of you who have been through it never believed that would be the outcome for you either. When you look at the last two situations I went through, I wouldn't believe a cop would rape me either. They are supposed to protect and serve. Who do you trust?

There have been several times I had to stop writing because I have been overwhelmed emotionally. All these secrets we keep for years balled-up inside of us eventually explode. I believed it was true that I wasn't going to amount to ANYTHING. How do you keep recovering when you constantly get knocked down? How do you feel special when the results of your life tell you otherwise? I've replayed the comment I heard from my high school guidance counselor when I said I didn't want to attend college. Her voice stayed with me for many years, trying to validate my existence. Let this be a lesson for ALL of us. We don't know how our words will affect people throughout their life. Let us make a point to breathe positive encouragement to others and not gossip or breed negativity. Find what's right with everyone instead of what's wrong them.

I continued to pick up protein powder for the boys in

Life in the Jetstream

London. Victor was kind enough to introduce me to the next set of guys coming in for several months. I hit it off with a guy named Rob Ashton. We all met at the infamous Stringfellow's. I found out Rob had previously worked with the airline that I was with for about four months in San Francisco. Now, he's a Chippendale touring Europe. He kept me sane in London for the next few months. We would go dancing, to the movies, riding bumper cars, to the gym, and I would head to the shows with him as often as I could.

Rob and I never dated because he reminded me of one of my brothers. We had a lot of fun. I loved that he was nice to everyone. He was always concerned about his appearance, which was part of his job. He did like the finer things in life. His mother flew to London to see him and do some sightseeing. He asked if I would help entertain her with him. Of course, I would. She thoroughly enjoyed the city. I was able to get out and see some things I wouldn't normally see. The night before she left Rob wanted to take her dancing. We headed out on the town. It was a bit funny because she got really mad at him for talking to other girls. I assured her it was fine and that we were only friends. She thought he was being extremely rude. We saw her off, and I headed to LA for my trip. After the last fiasco in New York,

Chapter 7

I chose not to fly there for several months.

On my trip back to London from LA, we had a band on board called W.A.S.P. I was working first class so I didn't see or talk to them throughout the flight. We had met briefly at the end of the flight. They were gracious enough to invite us ALL to Donnington Castle for The Monsters of Rock Concert in 1992. It is AMAZING that we get so many invites for some of the most interesting events, shows, and parties. So for those of you who offer invitations out of kindness, many times we will take you up on the offer. Flight attendants are very adventurous, so don't invite us if you really don't mean it. I thought it was an awesome gesture to go to the show, but there weren't any trains going there. I solely relied on public transport. I told the crew if they decided to go, to let me know. I went to bed, and later Jenny gave me a call saying they were going to the show. I was off for the next few days, so I said okay pick me up. It was an hour and a half from London.

When we were driving up to the event, people were everywhere. The stage was massive. It was unbelievable that all these people were in no man's land. I thought the manager was just getting us into the show. When we arrived, they let us in the back where all the bands have different trailers set up for the show. We had to get VIP passes to stay backstage. The guys came over and said hello and seemed so happy to see the crew. They were like, "WOW we didn't think you would come." This really was my first time officially meeting them. The guys had said good-bye while leaving first class on the airplane, but that was all.

Johnny Rod was one of the band members. That was his stage name. He asked if he could show me around. I said sure. He first took me to the HUGE catering tent. I didn't know who Sebastian Bach was at the time, but he was TRASHED, yelling, making a fool of himself, and breaking liquor bottles. This was way before the show even started. John was explaining every aspect of who, what, where, and how it all worked. It was very interesting. Working for East Coast Entertainment was more like club shows, weddings, and TGIF's not necessarily BIG venues like this.

I was NOT a rocker. I did like all kinds of music, but couldn't tell you who any one artist was. I knew much more country music than anything else at the time. I had never heard of W.A.S.P. and meeting Blackie, the lead singer, was uncomfortable. Not the most personable person

Chapter 7

you'll ever meet. John made me feel right at home. I went back with the crew and we felt the crowds roar. It was so much fun. At the end of all the shows, there was a fireworks display that was SPECTACULAR. We all stood around in amazement. It was beautiful.

We all went and partied at their hotel till dawn. We went into the swimming pool and were doing some pretty juvenile things. We all exchanged numbers as we were leaving. They said they would be in London the next few days. It was a long drive back. We were exhausted. I hadn't pulled an all-nighter in a long time. I got back to my flat and was taking a long nap, when my phone rang. It was John calling to see what we all were doing that night. The band decided to come to London earlier. They mentioned Stringfellow's, and I said, "Great, I know the place well." He asked if he could come to my flat, and we'd go together. I said okay.

The band came in a white van and dropped him off at my flat that afternoon. It was much earlier than I expected. I was a bit nervous because I had NEVER brought guys to my flat. My landlady Devinder, was an amazing woman, but she might think it was inappropriate. I was thinking: what are we going to do until it's time to go clubbing? I

113

thought he was going to come by much later. I called my flying partner, Jenny, and we made a plan. Once again we had another fun-filled night of dancing and entertainment. The next day we toured the city around Covent Garden.

I ended up going to many European destinations with John during their tour. He was definitely NOT my type, but he was spontaneous and adventurous. He was loud and obnoxious and he made me laugh a lot. I never knew what would happen next. They were playing at the Élysée Montmartre in Paris. I flew in to meet him. They had to leave after the show in order to arrive at their next destination on time. The room was paid for, so I decided to stay. I would leave first thing in the morning.

I fell asleep and woke up to a man standing beside my bed speaking French to me. I was yelling, "GET OUT!" There were not any secondary locks to keep anyone out. He left, but about 20 minutes later, he was knocking on my door again. He wanted me to pay for being in the room. In Europe, they charge each person to stay, but because there was nobody else there, I took the room. I was frightened and couldn't go back to sleep no matter how many things I put against the door. It was definitely something I didn't want to experience again. I did see management the next

Chapter 7

morning. We had communication issues, so I finally just left. I live out of hotels, and it had never occurred to me that a man would be standing by my bed watching me sleep without me hearing him come in.

We also did the U.S. tour, and John even came to my hometown in Martinsville and met my brothers, Mark and Scott. My ex-boyfriend Ricky found out he was in town with me and called. Ricky was into heavy metal and rock. My brother Scott and Ricky ended up following us to the next show in Virginia Beach. I took my girlfriend Jennifer with us. We later went on to New York, DC, Pittsburgh, and Chicago, touring the cities. We took the ferry, went to the towers, and met a lot of other bands, like Dee Snider from Twister Sister in the NY venue. We sat at cafés and watched musicians play. It was certainly a whirlwind experience for me.

It is a lonely life on the road. The guys hurry up and wait. There is a lot of sitting around and calling loved ones or friends. There is one hotel after another, more venues, and lots of people who want a piece of you. Being a flight attendant, I was flexible to come and go. It is not the case when you are on tour. Life comes to a halt and you make the best of it. It reminded me of Steve Perry's song in his video, Faithfully. He's starring out the window of the bus, looks lonely and quiet. Its grey outside, with fields as far as the eye can see. It's sad to a certain extent. Yet I could relate. When bands are on tour they miss out on life that is happening elsewhere. Family births, deaths, sickness, celebrations, parties, activities and a little more of their life passes them by. Most only see the fun, radical, and adventurous life being played out on the road with adoring fans.

We were in Germany for a show, but soon after I arrived, John was upset. He told me previously that he was divorced with a daughter. I even talked to the "ex-wife." She said he was lying to me and that they were still married. I didn't know whom to believe. My first thought was: how sad, the mother of his child wants to reunite with him. I wondered if she knew what he was doing. Why would she want to stay with someone like that? He assured me it was OVER. However, it seemed like we were arguing over silly things, and I could never figure out why.

He asked me to go to Asia with him when they were touring in Japan. I knew something was happening; but thought I would take this final trip to see what the truth really was. It's interesting how things happen. I was in the

Chapter 7

boarding area in LA getting ready to board my flight to Tokyo. I met a few guys and a girl on the trip. They said they were in a band touring over there as well. They asked if I knew who, FIREHOUSE was. I said no.

We all took our seats and I was completely exhausted from flying from London, LA then to Tokyo, so I decided to take a rest. It was perfect. I had 5 seats together in economy to lie down flat. We were traveling on a 747. When I woke up, the guitarist of Firehouse, Bill Leverty, was walking by and said he had some of their music I could listen to. He sat down and I listened to the first song on the CD. I then knew exactly who they were. This was 1992 and they were at the top of the charts with "Love of a Lifetime." Bill was very kind and soft-spoken. He was nothing like many of the "rock stars" I had met along the way. He even helped me gather red wine for John as the flight attendants came through the aisle multiple times. I didn't even remember having one cocktail on the flight for myself.

I met CJ Snare, the lead singer of the band. He was with his wife, Kelly, who at the time was pregnant with their daughter. They asked what was bringing me to Narita. I told them I was going to see the guy I was dating, who was on tour there as well. After talking, we realized we were all

117

staying at the same hotel, The Roppongi Prince Hotel. They offered me a ride in their limo to the city. I was grateful because I knew it was going to be difficult to use public transportation to get there. It would have taken me three times longer doing it that way. They asked if I would come see one of their shows, and I said I'd love to. We exchanged names and phone numbers. I told them I would let them know what room I was in when we got there. Interesting enough, John was waiting in the lobby for me. When he watched me get out of the limo with them, he was less than excited.

John was acting like a jerk. I told them all it was really nice meeting them and thanks for the ride. They asked me again in front of John if I could go to one of their shows. I blurted out, "Let's check out which nights we're free." Kelly said, "You go to ALL of their shows, you can come by yourself." I said that would be great. John was pissed off. As we walked away, he kept calling them "Firehose." I told him he should appreciate them giving me a ride. It would have taken me at least two hours longer without them. I was safe and he should be thanking them.

He calmed down a bit and the plan that night was to go to Queens Way. It seemed like several of the guys from both bands and roadies showed up for a night to dance and party before the tour got started. We danced so much we were drenched. It was nice running into Michael, the drummer, and Bill, the guitarist of Firehouse at the club. John was more at ease then. It could have been the alcohol talking. Who knows!

I believe we had a show the next night. We spent the day touring Tokyo. We went by the Hard Rock Café and bought some shirts. The music stores were unreal. You could listen to the albums before you bought them. That was way before the U.S. incorporated that system. I couldn't believe they had beer machines, just like a soda machine out on the sidewalks. I remember the streets being very crowded. I felt really tall, and I was starred at constantly with my blonde hair. I loved going to their shows. Asians just LOVE their metal bands. There was energy like no other. I believe we had done 3 shows by then.

I was dyeing John's hair bleach blonde in the hotel room when one of the guys from Firehouse called. Bill asked if I was going to be able to come see them play. I told him I'd call back. Timing wasn't the best at that moment. John went nuts again. It was in that moment that I knew something was very wrong. Of course, I was not able to go see one of their shows while I was in Japan. It seems I was starting to repeat the same old patterns. I told myself: you don't have to put up with this. You can walk away anytime.

That night I wanted to go dancing again. John was tired and wanted to stay in. I didn't want to sit around after flying half way around the world. I knew this was probably the last time I would see John, and I wanted to do what I wanted to do. I really wanted to get to the bottom of what was going on with us. I felt the relationship was over; I just needed to confirm it. That night I snuck out of the room to go dancing. It was just around the corner, and I knew the W.A.S.P road crew would be there to keep an eye on me. I also knew John couldn't get jealous because the Firehouse guys were doing a show. That still didn't go over too well, of course. What it did do was bring everything to a head.

John locked me out of the room and I had to go his friend's room who was another band member. There were two guys from the band and one guy from the crew who were in there talking about what was happening. They alluded to me that John was not being completely honest with me anyway. They told me I was too nice and he didn't

Chapter 7

deserve me. At this point, I said to myself: what the heck are you thinking, Toni? He's still married isn't he? They wouldn't confirm it, but I knew. That's all I needed to walk away.

I told John I needed to get my things and I wanted to head home. I started packing, and he asked if I would stay one more day. I wanted to close this chapter and find out the truth. I started asking him questions without letting him know the guys had said anything. He never led on until I went to get coffee downstairs. I came back to the room and he was now questioning me about talking to his "ex." I had not talked to her since Germany. By this time, it was too late for me to take the flight back until the next day. I knew in my heart at that point that he was lying and still married. Why would he be so worried about me talking to his ex-wife? It seemed his insecurities had gotten the best of him.

I later found out that his good friend, another band member, was calling his wife every time I came to meet him. He was trying to make up and being nice, realizing I had no idea what he was talking about. It was like a switch turned off for me. I did go to their show again one last time. I was disappointed and heartbroken. I looked at all the time I had been around everyone in the band and the crew,

121

toured all over the world, met a lot of industry people, and it was just a HOAX. I knew when I left early the next day that it would be the last time I saw or spoke to him.

I did not see him again, but I did want closure. I wrote a letter on my flight home to his "wife." I said that I would be at this Florida hotel on this day. She was in Venice, California. I told her if it was really true and they were still married, to call me on this day and at this time and I would walk away completely. She did! I felt so betrayed. Why would a grown man lie to me like that and lead a completely separate life? Needless to say, I got the information I needed. I also found out she tried to get me fired from my job saying that I was carrying drugs for both bands to Tokyo. You never know to what extent someone is willing to go to hurt others. It doesn't take away the hurt, pain, and mistrust.

Another life lesson revealed. Just like Chris Rock says in his show, "We are only as honest as our options." In my line of work, we meet a lot of people who travel and are away often. I look back at relationships, when the writing was clearly on the wall. Here's how to recognize if someone is not being completely honest. When someone says do not pick up their hotel phone, when they give you a

Chapter 7

friend's number or email address to keep in touch with them, when you don't get a home phone number, when you are never invited to their personal home or when they would rather have room service than go out. Today, people are silly with social media and camera's everywhere. You can find out way more than you need to know. Those are a few indications to run the other way. Living on the road we do things differently. If you have to ask if something is right or not, listen to your intuition.

A few days later, I worked another trip to LA after the Chippendale tour. The guys had to go back to Los Angeles and learn new dance numbers and routines for the next tour. After a day of rehearsals, my girlfriend, Kerri, who was now living in LA, met me in her truck and we went to pick up Rob Ashton for dinner. About six of the guys jumped in the back of her truck and we headed to Hard Rock Café at the Beverly Center. As we sat down, I noticed Charlie Sheen was sitting with his entourage at the restaurant. I told Rob that Charlie and a friend were on my flight to London, where he was promoting a film. Toward the end of the flight, he and his friend asked my flying partner and me out while they were in London. I respectfully declined due to other obligations. However, the other flight attendant did take his friend up on the offer.

123

It was only a brief encounter, but Rob challenged me to see if Charlie would remember me. In my head, I knew that there wasn't a chance, but I'm always up for a challenge. I walked over to his table. He started smiling and immediately asked, "What are you doing in LA?" That could have been a blanket greeting, who knows, but I didn't care. I told him I was seeing some friends and house hunting. He said he had a great place in Malibu. I laughed. I told him I already checked out a place in Malibu. He then asked, "What are you doing with the Chippendales?" I said I was hanging out with my friends. I was shocked that he would know who they were. He waved to everyone. It was hilarious, so I got my laugh.

I went back to the table and had dinner. When we finished, the next thing I knew, the staff was coming to our table, clapping and singing, "Happy Birthday." I was looking around to see whose birthday it was. The staff brought ME the dessert and commemorative Hard Rock glass. I looked at Rob and he was laughing so hard he fell out of his chair. My face turned beet red. He got the last laugh this time. I still have that commemorative glass and cherish it to this day.

This was a crucial time for the Chippendales because

Chapter 7

their owner, Steve Banerjee, had just been put in jail for plotting to have one of the Adonis guys killed. Adonis was formed by previous Chippendales, and they took their secrets to Europe to branch out on their own. I was sitting with about 10 of the guys at a hotel in LA waiting for the show Hard Copy to come on. The guys were uncertain about their fate and wanted to hear the latest news.

The show came on and basically said that Steve was in jail awaiting trial for the allegations named above. I had met Steve on several occasions. He was always kind and generous to me. He treated me with respect, and he was a family man. I couldn't believe what was happening. What drives someone to do these things? A few months later in October 1994, Steve committed suicide while being detained in the county jail. The VP of Chippendale's corporation, Bob Greene, took over daily activities for the company.

Rob became my closest friend. I stayed in the city with him when I was back in London. I decided to have my best friend's; Jennifer and Kerri come and visit me in London. What I didn't tell them was that we were staying at the Chippendale hotel. The guys had massive flats, which is unheard of in Europe. Rob thought they would like the

125

Life in the Jetstream

adventure. My flat was close to the airport and extremely tiny. It was a cool idea and they loved it. All of the Chippendales on tour wanted to have a BIG PARTY before going away. They each had their own invitation list. The guys did a fabulous job getting everything for the party. The only task the girls had was to decorate and to find someone to cover the entrance door so that ONLY people on the guest list would get in.

I decided to cook dinner before the night got started. Boy was that hilarious. I know I made chicken, but I think I poured the entire can of pepper on it. It really wasn't edible, but Rob managed to eat quite a bit. The girls just laughed at me. They already knew I wasn't Betty Crocker. We started getting ready for the party and there were 4 guys and 4 girls in this one flat with ONLY two bathrooms. The dynamics were interesting.

Normally it takes the girls longer to get ready, but not in a Chippendale household. Jennifer and I had a conversation as we were getting ready for the party. We decided that one year from today, Jen would move to Los Angeles and I would commute from London to be there as well. When you come from a small town, it's easy to fall in the trap and settle for mediocrity. This is only because you can't have the same experiences as much bigger cities offer. Our conversation was about choosing to follow a dream and broadening her horizons.

We turned up the music and the party got started. We blew up so many balloons and had streamers everywhere. The place was hopping, everyone dancing, several floors of people. Rob was never a BIG drinker at all, but this night he decided to tie one on. Why this night? I don't know. The girls were meeting new people; talking to the guys we didn't see so much. It was great having my friends there with me.

I remember being on the second floor, and the main party was on the third. I was talking to one of the other guys from the show. I never really talked to him much until this night. He didn't drink much either so he was staying low-key. My girlfriend, Jen comes down to tell me Rob was upset. I said," Why?"

"He knows you are talking to Charles." She answered.

I responded, "So."

She stated, "He's really intoxicated and you need to come upstairs to talk to him."

I told her, "I'll be right up."

I went upstairs to the kitchen. It was full of people. He asked if I would go to the terrace with him. I said, "What's wrong with you?" That's when the flood gates opened up and he told me that he cared about me all along and wanted more than a friendship. I told him that we had talked about that already. I'd watched him with another girlfriend with whom I got along great. Next another old flame showed up, asking if he'd pose in his briefs with her. She had posed for Playboy at some point, on the cover of what's considered a trashy magazine. An article in The Sun came out, and they were half-naked saying they were the perfect couple. Rob just laughed at it. When Rob and I first met, it was a possibility. The more we got to know each other, the stronger the friendship had gotten. Relationships ruin friendships. I was only learning what it meant to be a good friend.

I didn't date guys from London or ones who lived locally. It would have made sense, but it never seemed to work out that way. I was able to spend a lot of time with Rob. I had no idea he felt that way about me. I truly loved him as a friend. I gave him a hug that night and told him we'd talk about it the next day. We hung out together the

Chapter 7

rest of the night. I knew by morning he wouldn't say much about it. The alcohol was doing the talking as it ALWAYS does in EVERY situation.

The next day, in London we had another BIG day in store. I had a friend get all of us free tickets to the All-American Bowl between the Washington Redskins and San Francisco 49ers. It was June 24th 1992. I'm not much of a football fan, but it was exciting! This was the largest crowd they had ever had in history. I was together with my best friends, Rob, Jen, and Kerri. Rob loved being with three other women. It certainly was another day to remember. The next night I couldn't let the girls go home without seeing an official Chippendale show and hanging out at our favorite night spot. Their trip had come to an end, and it was time to say good-bye. I had such a great time with them. I didn't want it to end.

I received a call from Bill Leverty of Firehouse about a month after I left Tokyo. It was such a surprise. I was in London between trips, and he said they would be touring in the UK. I said it so happens I will be able to attend the show this time. We laughed because I never realized going to Japan was going to turn out the way it did. I went to Wales to see the first show. The music was much more of my style. It was not nearly as heavy as W.A.S.P.'s CJ's voice was clean and crisp. His wife Kelly and I hit it off from the start. The next day, she and I decided to get on the train and head back to London.

The guys would be coming later. We had an enjoyable ride, seeing a bit of England's countryside. We talked about how my relationship with John ended in Japan. I loved her spunk. She said John wasn't good enough anyway. How can everyone see what you can't? She checked into her hotel and we were off to Hard Rock Café for dinner. We made plans to meet the next day. They were doing a show at Wembley Arena with a band called Status Quo. Another awesome show! There is a rush in the midst of a massive concert venue, screaming fans, everyone singing their songs. CJ, Bill, and Michael were so down to earth. They have always to this day stayed humble and given their fans exactly what they wanted, which is more of themselves. They give their all in every show and spend hours taking photos and giving autographs to their fans.

The next day, they were all flying to New York on my airline for the American Music Awards. I went with them to the airport to say good-bye. They wanted me to go with them on the flight. I was always up for an adventure, but I

Chapter 7

only had one more day off. I was a bit panicky. Finally, I had the agent put me on the flight and booked a return trip within three hours. The flight attendants were very hospitable and fun which made it memorable for all of us. I can't say I've ever done that again.

A long-term relationship was created in that short time. I stayed in touch often with them. I even met CJ and Kelly, in Los Angeles when they were recording their next album. I babysat their daughter, we showed CJ's mom around LA, and we had a great night out on the town at Miso. They lived in Florida when I was in between London and Los Angeles.

When I went back to Los Angeles, my favorite hangout was the infamous Roxbury. My girlfriend Jen did make the move from Martinsville to Los Angeles a year later? It was not easy making the transition. Her family was not supportive of her moving out to LA initially. I was still living in London and commuting to LA. My mother, my brother Scott, and Jen, drove my car and hers to California. I was on eggshells and tense because I had not found affordable housing for us yet. We didn't have much money, but I looked at several options. Luckily, I had a good friend, Bobby, who watched me stress out over her coming and not

131

having proper arrangements.

Bobby had an extra home in Encino, right near Mulholland Drive. If you know anything about LA, it's a pricey but beautiful area. He was going to allow us to use his home until we got on our feet. I just had to help him clean it up from his previous tenants. To this day, I'm forever grateful for his help. It was seriously a life saver for us.

I remember the few weeks before Jen moved to LA, I was working with Central/Cenex casting. I was on the Paramount studios lot doing extra work for the movie, "Falling Angels." It was a treat. I was dressed in a beautiful, sleek 50's gown. We had to actually get our hair and make-up done to set the scene. It was a glamorous look. I had a dance partner for the entire day, not just this scene. We had about an hour and a half left to film when something happened that left me puzzled.

This next scene was of James Woods walking by, and he takes the photographer's camera and slams it to the ground. Immediately, he starts yelling at me asking, "Where have you been all day?"

I said, "Right here."

Chapter 7

You could have heard a pin drop. There were about 200 people in the room. I was freaking out. I said to my dance partner, "Tell him I have been here all day." When you are on set there are TWO major things you do not do. Don't piss off the director or the stars of the show in any way. They'll always get their way. Stay clear. Let them do their job. My mind was racing thinking they are going to remove me from the set. I wouldn't get paid and the day would be lost.

We finally had a break and I went out of the studio onto this deck outside where there were very few people hanging out. I was taking a breath of somewhat fresh air and getting over my panic mode. What do you know; James Woods comes out on the deck. I wanted to leave, but thought it would be too noticeable. He starts talking, and I'm looking around to see who he was talking to. I don't remember his exact comments, but I do remember saying, "I never liked you since watching, "The Onion Field." He said, "Your mother shouldn't have let you watch it anyway." I had to laugh then. It broke the ice because I was extremely stressed. He said he was kidding with me in there. I said it wasn't appreciated. We talked for a few more minutes, and then it was time to start filming again.

Life in the Jetstream

Before I left, James, who liked to be called Jimmy, asked me to come over to where he was. He asked what I was working on next. I said I was on the Paramount lot tomorrow for Suzanne Pleshette's pilot. He said he was on the lot, too; maybe we could meet at the cafeteria. I said no problem and gave him my pager number. Yes, we had pagers then. Our shows didn't break at the same time, but he kept paging and paging me. When I finally got out at the end of the day, I called him back to apologize that it didn't work out. He said to call him sometime and gave me his home number. I had no intentions of calling him. I would have talked to him in the cafeteria, have lunch, but I wasn't interested. He had totally bruised my ego in front of 200 people.

When Bobby and I were cleaning up the house in Encino, my pager went off about three times. I wasn't calling back. Bobby said, "Who is it?" I told him what happened on the set and who it was. He said you have to call him back. I didn't want him to get the wrong idea. Bobby said just find out what he wants. I knew what he wanted, but Bobby said to call anyway. When I called, Jimmy invited me to dinner at Hamburger Hamlet in Beverly Hills. I said I couldn't go. I didn't have clothes to change into. I was filthy from cleaning the house, but he

134

Chapter 7

wouldn't take no for an answer. So I went. I didn't care about my appearance anyway.

It's kind of funny now. I drove up in my 1990 Ford Probe with missing hubcaps, which had been stolen, and he was right behind me in his black Porsche. We had dinner and talked quite a bit. He was much nicer and more laid back than I figured. This was about the time his father passed away. Timing was bad, but I thought: you can never have too many friends in LA. As we were leaving, he was trying to convince me to go bowling with him. He was on a league that he played on every week. I thought that was unusual, but it added some normalcy in his life. We stayed in touch here and there until the phone conversations got way out of hand. That's all I have to say about that.

However, I did later run into him at a star-studded event in 1993. I was invited to go to see the opening of Sunset Boulevard. I went with a well- known Ears, Nose & Throat specialist from Beverly Hills. Actually, I didn't know where I was going to begin with. The doctor just asked if I owned a cocktail dress and it went from there. He was going to have a car sent for me, but I told him I'd meet him at his place. When I got there, he proceeded to tell me we were picking up the hosts of the event. When he said their

135

Life in the Jetstream

names, I was oblivious. We stopped by to pick them up on our way to the theatre. They were a cute older couple known as Billy and Audry Wilder. He produced the 1950s film Sunset Boulevard.

When we arrived, I hadn't seen ANYTHING like this before in person. It was LIGHTS, CAMERAS, PEOPLE, and LONG RED CARPETS. I was terrified beyond belief. I had a nervous laugh and felt my legs were going to give out on me. So I practically ran down the aisle until Joe pulled me back. I was astonished. We were at the OPENING of Sunset Boulevard starring Glenn Close. Every celebrity you could think of was in that room. My first thought was if a bomb went off that night we would lose many of our treasured icons. I don't know why I would give that a thought. Elizabeth Taylor, Clint Eastwood, George Hamilton, Candice Bergen, Halle Berry, Patrick Swayze, and of course, James Woods were just a few in attendance. James was sitting directly in front of me. He turned around to see me sitting there and asks what I'm doing there. I said, the same reason he was to see the show. It's a small world.

Jen had made it to LA. We stayed in Encino, and within the week, she had a job in Beverly Hills. The first shopping

Chapter 7

trip was typical of college students paying their own way. We bought several packages of Ramen noodles and lots of macaroni and cheese. We weren't the most prepared, but we made it. We were at Bobby's house for two months before renting a room out of a beautiful home on Redondo Beach. We were able to start venturing out a bit more.

Ask Yourself:

Did you grow up putting celebrities on a pedestal? Did you dream of a life of traveling, celebrities, parties, and adventures? What did you dream of to escape reality? How did you think your life would turn out? Did you hold yourself accountable in situations that tempted you?

Life's Lessons:

I came from the poor side of town, so I did put celebrities on a pedestal because I thought their life was unattainable. I realized later that they are exactly like us. Living in London, I met more entertainers than local people. I went to all of the parties, had adventures, and met tons of celebrities. It was no more fulfilling than what my imagination led me to believe. I had a skewed sense of reality. However, I enjoyed the spontaneity. I enjoyed seeing and doing things I've never done before. It was intriguing! I was searching for love. I was lonely living in another country so I kept myself busy and entertained.

I was living what I thought was the dream life. Compared to where I came from, this was a DREAM, despite the unfortunate circumstances that came my way. Happiness is not an event or something someone can give you. It comes from within. When you have been able to do what everyone dreams of, you realize there is a bigger purpose to being here. It's your choice to make the best of any given situation. If you have heard the saying, "the grass is greener on the other side," think again.

Chapter 8

(Arriving at MY Destination)
Making a Change & Settling Down

IN MARCH 1994, I FLEW TO HAWAII FOR VACATION BY MYSELF. I originally had plans with a few flight attendants to go to Mexico. When the time came to go, it seemed no one had the money. Every year I would go to Hawaii. I knew the island, it was easy to meet new people, I always felt safe, and it had some amazing views. I was flying to meet friends in Maui who were dancers. I had met them as stunt guys for The Power Rangers in LA months before. They had a show to perform that night, and my flight came in just afterwards. We still headed out to go dancing and made a night of it. Their resort was stunning. The next day, we flew back to Oahu and they dropped me off in their limo at my hotel.

I headed to the beach soon after arriving to go see some other friends. I had a normal routine. I loved the international marketplace, because it was there when I had started my first business in 1989. I wanted to see what was new and unique. My night spots were Moose McGillycuddy's and Hernando's Hideaway. I'd lay on the

Life in the Jetstream

beach to catch a tan, than take the catamaran. It made the sun feel less intense because of the breeze. I made it a point to say hello to one of the guys that ran the Windjammer. They were always giving me a free ride. This massive catamaran sits in front of The Outrigger Reef Hotel closer to the marina. We always had a good time and made a lot of memories on that boat.

On my last day on the island, I had planned on taking the red-eye out that night. I had been talking to the guys from the catamaran before I started walking back to the hotel. I saw all of these Air Force guys around my girlfriend, Tammy who was a local bartender at The Outrigger Reef Hotel. I was washing the sand off my feet when two of the guys were standing nearby. The tall, dark, and handsome one said to me, "Why don't you come over here? The sun's better on this side." I immediately labeled him a PLAYER and walked away.

I hate guys using smooth lines as introductions. I had been around so many PLAYERS. I was NOT looking for a man at this time, even though I thought he was handsome. I was disappointed, and went to lie out in front of the hotel. All the guys took the catamaran ride. When they came back, Tammy spotted me on the beach and said, "I'm getting the

Chapter 8

guys their first drink. Come join us. I know you don't have anything better to do." I declined. She replied "You are coming with me. I can't be the only girl in this bunch." I saw the guy that gave me the line and cringed.

We all got a table outside on the beach. They introduced themselves and we talked about what we were doing in Hawaii, where we were from, and other trivial tidbits about our lives. The guy who sat next to me became so annoying. He kept asking me to go out with him that night every ten seconds. I was not interested at all. We had a few drinks and several jokes. It ended up being a decent visit despite the guy asking me out every ten seconds. The other guys said to just ignore him so I wouldn't leave.

That night they were going to have a party in their room. They were new to Oahu, so I told them to head to my favorite places. They were all asking me to stay and go with them. I wasn't pressed to go back to LA, but flights are always touch-and-go on standby. The tall, dark, and handsome guy, Rob, was with his friend and crew mate, Mark. Mark had such a soft-spoken voice and was a super nice guy. Rob didn't talk to me after I blew him off, but Mark would speak on his behalf, which was pretty amusing.

I was wearing a checkered red, black, and white shirt with jagged cut-off sleeves. It was way too big on me because Rob Ashton, my Chippendale friend was who gave it to me. Mark kept asking if his friend, Rob could have that shirt. I said no. I wasn't taking my shirt off with only my bikini on. I thought it was a trick. I was often paranoid about men and their motives during this time. I had every reason to be paranoid.

I started winding down and wanted to leave. Mark said the party was going to be in his room. The guys had huge suites with two rooms and two balconies overlooking the ocean. I told him I'd pop over for a bit, but I needed to be packed and ready to go that night. I went back to my hotel, which was only two blocks away, to shower and change. They said the party was starting at 7 p.m. I am not a girl to be fashionably late. My motto is, "One minute late and you miss the plane." For the most part, I was always on time or early, unless it was out of my control.

I was dressed and ready to go, so I headed over to the party. I was walking to Mark's room when here come's "Rob" with two other girls down the hall, not showered or dressed. I thought what a loser and yes, what a player. Guess all these guys are on Caribbean time. He dropped the

Chapter 8

girls and took me to Mark's room. I think there were five people in there to start. It was good because I had a chance to talk to them one-on-one. Rob wanted to talk to me on the other balcony where nobody was. I finally agreed to talk in the living room while the others were on the balcony.

Mark kept assuring me that Rob was a great guy. I trusted Mark for some reason. After talking for a while, more people were coming in. Rob wanted me to help him pick out his clothes that night. I refused. He was insistent that it would only take a minute to choose an outfit. I went to his room and he opened his closet. Guess what, only one outfit was hanging there. I told him, "You already have your answer," and walked out the door.

The party started and everyone was having a good time. Rob came back, and he apologized for earlier. I was waiting for the joke, but it didn't come. He ended up being really cordial. Everyone was heading to the first stop across the street for one drink. I don't know who bought that round for everyone, but I asked Rob if he'd drink the margarita they ordered for me. I wasn't a tequila drinker at all. I had to make a decision then to take the flight or stay one more night. I decided to stay. The crew was headed to Moose McGillycuddy's, and I suggested Rob and I head to

Hernando's Hideaway where it was low-key, then we would meet up with them later.

At Hernando's Hideaway, we had a chance to talk. There was an old jukebox playing. We decided to play the music we each liked. He talked about his family and his Air Force experience. I could see that he was different when he wasn't around the group. It was such a pleasant change from earlier. We then headed to meet everyone. We danced and had a few drinks. His demeanor certainly changed around others. He had to be the life of the party. Still very charming and attentive, but he was a busy bee making sure everyone was having a good time. I had about three drinks, knowing I should have stopped at two. We headed back to the hotel. Unfortunately, we both had too much to drink and I thought he was playing games with me. So I took off and ran away. This seemed to be my way of dealing with things.

We caught up with one another the next morning. He walked me to my limo that was headed to the airport. He took my number and address. He was heading to Okinawa, Japan and Singapore. I flew back to LA. This was March of 1994. Rob called two days later and asked if I would come back to Hawaii. I said I'd see what I could do. My

Chapter 8

girlfriend Kerri's dad lived there. Kerri was getting married to Simon Russell. Simon was the son of Graham from Air Supply. The three of us jumped on a flight to Honolulu where we spent time with her dad and hung-out. I had Kerri drop me off, where I was to meet Rob coming in from Singapore. He never showed up. I decided to stay the night at the same hotel I stayed at when we first met. It's so cliché about Hollywood movies.

It was about 2:30 a.m. my time when Rob called me in the SAME hotel from Singapore telling me the plane was broken. He said they were going to try to leave the next day. He didn't own a credit card, and once again, his friend, Mark came to the rescue and loaned him his to call me. I hooked up with Kerri and Simon for the day and tried to meet him again later. I left a note at the hotel for him and decided it was best for me to get back to LA. So I took the red- eye that night.

He arrived in Hawaii, soon after I left. When he got the note, he thought I was still there. It didn't work out then, but he called me to reschedule. We decided to meet up on the East Coast. I had to make an appearance at the 7th annual Miss Roanoke Teenager pageant because I was the 1st Miss Roanoke Teenager. I had a friend, Cathleen in

145

from LA who was a Raider's cheerleader and was judging the pageant as well. Rob wanted to come to the pageant then, but I knew I would be stressed in that environment. We had not even really been on a first date. We agreed that I would fly to DC for two days and leave from there to return to London.

I flew to DC, and luckily, Rob brought his friend Mark with him. I was relieved. As we were walking to the car, Rob asked if we could pick up some beer as we made a plan. I stopped dead in my tracks and said to Rob, "Do you ALWAYS drink?" He was taken aback by my response.

He said, "Oh no, we don't have to." Later, he admitted to me he was nervous and wanted to take the edge off. I was thinking immediately that I had enough alcoholics around me, and I wouldn't allow that. It was a totally different experience after visiting him. He was kind, gentle, attentive, great-natured, and he listened even more than he spoke. I found he had many characteristics I was looking for in a partner. Although I'd had it with men, Rob gave me hope that I could have the best of both worlds.

We were inseparable after that. I was sitting on a big decision that was underway. What I had to do then was

Chapter 8

figure out how NOT to go to Hong Kong. I had moved out of my flat in London and was supposed to move to Hong Kong to open a new base. I had changed my mind. Fortunately, after meeting Rob, the company wasn't ready to open the base after all. I was forced out of London because my three-year visa was expiring and I was eventually transferred to Washington, DC.

Rob and I started dating. It was humorous because he asked to speak to my mother when I was home visiting. I said, "WHY?" I finally put her on the phone, and he asked if I could come to visit him in Maryland. I remember it as if it were yesterday. She said, "Toni is 24 years old, she can do what she wants to." How sweet, but she's right. I made my own decisions. I think he was being a gentleman. Rob had the Ozzie & Harriett lifestyle. His dad had a great job when he was growing up, and his mother took care of the children, the cooking, and the cleaning. She would later get a job at the school to be nearby. They were surrounded by a lot of family and good times. His parents are still married now for over 50 years.

I use to tell Rob the stories about how I lived during my childhood. He could never grasp the concept. He thought I was a strong, independent, woman. I was, but the scars ran

147

deeper than anyone knew. I do recall right before we got married, Rob was visiting my family's home. My dad had his moody side. We were all having a conversation. Rob and I were in the living room on the couch, and Mom was standing up closer to the door. Dad had walked out of the room briefly. I guess Mom had interrupted him too much when he jerked down the light switch chain and hurled it at mom. I was shocked that he did it front of Rob. I don't think Rob believed me when I talked how my childhood really was. I was hoping Rob would get up and say something like, "You IDIOT," but we were all quiet. What do you say at a time like that? I was surprised Rob didn't run learning there might be some truth to my insanity.

It wasn't smooth sailing initially. My dad didn't like that Rob was of an ethnic background. The first thing Mom said in my ear when we arrived at night was, "Is he black?" It didn't help that he'd just come back from Egypt with his dark half-Puerto Rican skin. We also drove up in his 1985 Hoopty with a speaker so big it filled the back seat. He had something wrong with his car. After driving five hours, the right side passenger floor board was burning my shoes.

He always told everyone the story that he would look through a woman's purse or cabinets in the bathroom to make sure she was not taking drugs, on meds, or had anything that may be considered harmful. Wow! Do people do that? Was he being serious? I guess it's an idea. Not one I would recommend unless you are having doubts. Luckily, I passed with flying colors. It's not what you see on the outside that counts, it's what you can't see that he'll later have problems with.

Seriously, Rob and I were raised with two totally different backgrounds. It was going to be a challenge integrating the relationship. Rob and I married soon after. We did not have a clue what was in store for us. I initially loved being married. I had someone there to support me. Something I felt I truly needed. We have learned a lot together over the years. We had some great times, but it has also been a bumpy road. I think everyone goes through transition periods in their lives. I share my stories, hoping you'll relate with what has happened, is happening or might happen. We get the opportunity to change our circumstances.

When I was dating Rob, he wanted to buy a Toyota Supra. He was in the Air Force, so I thought he'd be able to get a loan for it. I was floored that he could serve our country and not get a loan. So I took a loan through my

Life in the Jetstream

credit union instead. He loved that car. After getting married and me becoming pregnant, two sports cars just weren't going to cut it. We were going to need a mini-van. He was not about to have any of that. He would NOT be a mini-van man.

I was getting closer to my due date with our first son. We needed to make a decision. He decided to sell his Supra. We received a call from someone interested in buying the car and I chose to sell it for less than Rob wanted. This became our first real fight. We'd had dinner at a Chinese restaurant earlier, and after we began to argue. I decided to sleep in the guest room that night. At about 7 a.m., I woke up to my water breaking. I walked into the bedroom where Rob was and told him to call the doctor, my water broke. I kept on walking to the bathroom to take a shower. Rob ran up to me and said, "Really, the baby's coming? Are we still friends?" It was so cute. I jumped in the shower before heading to the hospital.

He was the sweetest guy ever when Austin arrived. Austin was born at about 6:10 p.m. that night. The next day Rob went out to pick up what I needed after taking me home from the hospital. He wrote the most beautiful card I had ever received. He was accommodating and such a

Chapter 8

doting dad. We had to make some decisions we didn't like about our living situation. We had to live in a double-wide mobile home, but Rob had to sacrifice his weekend twice a month to mow the lawn in the park to pay for park fees. It was definitely not the ideal situation. As new parents you have to start somewhere.

Rob was working as a police officer in Prince George County, MD. I was still a flight attendant. It was time for me to go back to work. Trying to find child-care was unsettling, though we did have a family friend that helped us tremendously. I was based in Miami now, so I had to commute. I was unhappy commuting, going to work, coming home, and trying to have a life. I told Rob we needed to move to Florida. He could be a police officer there. We sold our place and went to Florida when Austin was 7 months old. Rob went through the interview process and later got hired.

We built my DREAM home in Palm Beach, although Rob did not want to build at first. He was worried we couldn't afford it. I found an up-and-coming area and felt it was a good decision. We were now making good money. This was the first time I thought we could relax a bit after stressing for the first few years.

I remember that after we moved into our West Palm Beach home, something happened that tested my temper. Rob was still working as a police officer with Broward Sheriff's Department where the TV show, Cops was created. He had been working all day and was headed home for dinner. I felt like a great wife. I was so proud of myself for getting his dinner on the table when he had arrived home. I prepared spaghetti in meat sauce with garlic bread. He went to take the first bite and I was just staring at him with a big smile. Then, to my surprise, he spits it out and proceeds to dump the entire pot in the garbage. I don't know about you, but the feelings in my body went through the roof.

I was processing the information given and deciding my best way to respond. Given my childhood, I can only remember throwing, punching, and breaking things. There was also screaming, cursing, and accusing each other of bad behavior. In an instant, my thoughts were to throw something. I paused because I knew if I broke something, I had to pay to fix it. My dad paid to fix many things. I picked up a large plastic bowl and flung it at Rob toward the sliding glass doors where we entered the pool. He turned and looked as if I had two heads. I went from being madder than hell, to feeling like a wounded child in an

Chapter 8

instant. I was able to convey that I was so mad and hurt because he wasted good food. He obviously had never gone a day without a meal in his life. I had been hungry many times. That behavior was not acceptable. He said I should have learned to spice the food. I'd never had a cooking class in my life. I guess he could tell. We talked about me not knowing how to cook before we married, but I believe it fell on deaf ears.

What he did was send a message loud and clear that we would not agree or relate on this issue. I made it clear how I felt about throwing away food, and he made it clear we were not going to act out by throwing things or having temper tantrums like your 2 years old. Does that solve the problem? Not really. We spent years learning what each one could handle or are willing to put up with. When you are aware of your boundaries before-hand, more than likely these things don't happen often. We can laugh about it now, but it was very serious back then.

Later in life when Oprah had her TV show, she helped many women realize they weren't alone by talking about the sexual abuse she had suffered. Words you didn't utter became a healing ground for men and women all over the world. I was about 21 when I remember talking about my abuse for the first time. I brought the subject up to my cousin, Michelle, whom I adored. I knew she was still close to this family after all of these years. When I moved away, I only tried to forget. I had not asked her directly if she was abused by the same guy. I only wanted to see if she would talk about it when I brought it up. She didn't. I could tell she was uncomfortable.

It wasn't until I had my first son that I could muster the courage to ask her about Jeff, my abuser. I was shocked and dumbfounded when she said she was also abused and knew that her good friend, Jenny, was as well. She told me he had daughters, and I got even angrier. I had years to stew over my abuse alone. When I found out that there were three of us and he had daughters, I wanted to stop him. I wanted revenge and retaliation, not for myself but because I knew in most cases, once an abuser, always an abuser. I wanted to take him to court and file charges so he couldn't do it to anyone else. I felt guilty that I hadn't done anything before this. It's easier to try to just to get over it.

When I asked my cousin if she would do this with me, she was hesitant. She had stayed in the same town, and Jeff had even gone to her wedding. I was beside myself when she told me that. I was speechless. I told her she would never know how strongly you could feel about something like this, until you had kids of your own. We allow ourselves to go through situations that we'd never allow people we love to go through. We have conditions on love for ourselves.

It didn't help that bringing this situation up after so many years made the family uncomfortable. It seemed okay when everything was brushed under the carpet. Nobody wanted this secret to come into the light, for obvious reasons. They were worried his mother would have a heart attack with this information and wondered why we would even want to talk about it again after all of these years. You can't change the past.

Michelle later agreed to help me prosecute him after she had her first son. She was pregnant when we spoke about it again. She was 28 years old, getting ready to deliver her son, and she ended up in the hospital with pneumonia. I called the hospital to check on her. Austin was just a toddler and I lived three and a half hours away in Palm Beach, Florida. I talked to the nurse to make sure that Michelle would be okay and that I could come visit her after she had the baby. We had a scheduled trip to go to Virginia for a family photo, so I flew home. In a matter of two days, her lung collapsed, she got a staph infection, and she was flown to another hospital. She died without ever even holding her son. He did survive.

Talk about your world turning upside down. I was in disbelief. This doesn't happen anymore. How can that happen? I felt guilty as if part of it were my fault. I was and still am a big believer in signs. Signs show up everywhere, in the words people say, books you read, shows you watch, subtle hints around your house or someone else's. They could be anywhere. I needed to live with the fact that I wanted her to help me so badly and now she wasn't even here to enjoy her life or her son. I felt so selfish. I stepped back to reevaluate what I should do.

Michelle was a bright light in this dark world. She was always happy to see me and loved me unconditionally. She had a beautiful smile and there was such innocence about her. About two months before she passed away, she sent me a beautiful card with a pack of flowers to plant. I still have both the card and the pack of flowers, which I like to pick up every now and then as a constant reminder to never forget. They were Forget-Me-Not's. She may have passed on, but her memory will live on forever.

Chapter 8

It took many years for me to forgive myself for carrying part of that load. I never prosecuted my abuser. I had to learn to forgive first. I did try to find him on several occasions. As you read on, finding balance takes time, and learning to evolve in the midst of turmoil has its own challenges. We can be free and fulfilled if we give ourselves a chance.

It was about three and a half years into my marriage and I received devastating news about my ex-boyfriend Ricky. My brother Scott and his wife were staying with us in Palm Beach when my brother heard from a friend that Ricky had been murdered. Of course, no one knew the details about what happened. I decided to call and ask. I was extremely upset and did not believe it was true. He had so much tragedy in his life, and he'd thought he was invincible. I believed that. When my husband came home from work, he could see I was distraught. I told him what had happened and asked if he wanted to go to the funeral with me. He declined and thought I shouldn't go as well.

I knew I had to see him to close that chapter of my life. You may think that if you married to someone else, why you would have such strong feelings about this. I was a broken, a wounded woman trying to find my way. I had no business getting married because I didn't understand myself, let alone know how to deal with someone else. I walked away from the relationship with Ricky because the path was too destructive, not because I didn't care about him. I didn't really say good-bye, so I did what I knew best, ran away. I did not face it, nor did I communicate how I was feeling. This was hard for Rob to understand. My thoughts were the man is dead; he had nothing to worry about. I just NEEDED to do this for my own sanity. Closure is very important.

It's hard for people to understand what you're going through when something like this happens. I know I couldn't possibly understand why Rob would feel like I shouldn't go. Mostly, I believe he felt it was a lack of respect or dishonoring to him. In my heart, it was nothing like that.

I was pregnant with my second son, Kieran, during this time. Within six months after having my son, I fell into a deep depression. You hear people talk about postpartum depression, but before you experience it yourself, you wonder if it is real. It's very real and often misunderstood! Although my depression was only for a short period of time, I felt as if I were CRAZY.

Chapter 8

I was overwhelmed, irrational, and emotional. My plan was to pack my bags and leave without letting ANYONE know where I was going. It wasn't as if my children were in danger or I wanted to harm them, as I've heard from other stories. I just wanted out. Leave and not come back till I could handle life again. It may sound selfish and unreasonable, but the depths of despair will cause you to do things you never thought possible.

My husband noticed something was wrong with me. I can't seem to tell you what my behavior was. I was overtired, stressed, and depressed. It was hard to do anything right. I was a zombie. I was there physically, but just going through the motions. My mind was elsewhere. Rob sat me down and asked how he could help. I remember asking if he could give the kids a bath, make and clean up dinner for a few days, so I could catch up on some rest. It wasn't that he didn't help around the house; I just couldn't understand why I wanted to run, scream, and go to a quiet place. He helped me get through it. Believe it or not, that did the trick. I was back to normal again.

I was doing some work for several different charities at the time in 1996. My friend Rob Ashton, the Chippendale was on the cover of several True Romance novels. He

Life in the Jetstream

wanted to be the next Fabio. He came to do a fundraiser in Palm Beach for the Adam Walsh Children's Fund. My Nana was down for a visit when he flew in. She knew all of our stories of Rob. She acted like a schoolgirl when they met. It was hilarious to see because this is a woman I admired for her grace and elegance.

I was working a trip from Santiago, Chile when my flight cancelled, so I wasn't going to be able to pick Rob up from the airport. When you're a flight attendant, the best way to ensure a cancelled flight is to make concrete plans. This was the first time my husband would be meeting him in person. Of course, he knew all about him, but they had never met face-to-face. The problem was, my husband had gotten off work in Fort Lauderdale at Broward's Sheriff's Department, and then drove to Palm Beach only to turn around and go back to Fort Lauderdale that night. My husband pulled up about midnight and he didn't recognize Rob from the pictures. He said he thought he was a bum sitting on the ground, covered with an army jacket and a hood over his head.

I flew in the next morning. I barely had enough time to change and greet him. We had a radio interview to do. We jumped in the car and raced to get there. We could hear

Chapter 8

them saying he was missing in action. I had to call the radio station to explain the dilemma. We were about 15 minutes off schedule. The interview went great. All the girls on the staff wanted photos, and then we were off to the television station for another interview. We had a blast; everyone loved him. One of the radio hosts invited us out to give a tour of the Palm Beach night-life. Both Rob's are muscular, dark haired, and have olive skin. My best friend Rob asked my husband when we went out that night to wear long sleeves. He didn't want him capturing the spotlight. Overall, it was a memorable time for me. I wish I had known it would be the last time I'd see Rob Ashton.

I wouldn't normally treasure something so trivial like the Hard Rock Café glass he gave me years earlier. While he was in his thirties, Rob passed away to kidney failure. After speaking to his mother, she said he had a few close calls before with pneumonia, but he couldn't battle any longer. When I found out about his death, I cried for three days. My husband gave me the space I needed to grieve his passing. He had a larger than life personality and a soul taken way too soon. I have so many wonderful memories of our friendship and if you have ever lost anyone you know they always leave a footprint in your heart.

Later, I can remember a time when my husband and I were discussing my past. The idea was to help me move past some of my behaviors. We came to the conclusion about the way I chose the men in my life. I dated older, stronger, extremely masculine men. For the most part, they were secure with themselves, body-building types, if not fighters. I chose those men because I was looking for someone to protect me. I was reaching out for what I lacked growing up, thinking that someone else could provide that for me. I didn't know the answers were already inside of me.

Only about 5 years ago, my husband and I attended a theme party with our friends in Lynchburg, VA. We have been to several theme parties over the years with Randy and Natalie. This year we were going as Star Trek security guards in the red suits. I decided to jump in the shower. The suits had arrived, and Rob wanted to show me how they looked. He's just a big kid himself and one of the many reasons I love him. I stepped out of the shower, and he popped around the corner with his suit on in his guard stance, pointing a gun at me. I stood like a deer in the headlights and he noticed something was wrong. I began to cry. What had happened? Faced with a past memory of being shot, I disassociated, until I was faced with the trauma once again. I don't know what you have faced in your life, but if you have had trauma you will deal with it throughout your life. You just need to know its part of the process to heal.

Ask Yourself:

Did you ever imagine your ideal partner? What characteristics did he or she have? Are there things you haven't faced because of what you fear will happen? Are you choosing to suppress certain events in your life? Is there something or someone in your life that, you are pinning the responsibility of your happiness on? Have you had a loss in your life that you have had a hard time getting over? Have you gotten the closure you needed? Are you still grieving the loss of a friend or a loved one?

Life's Lessons:

I didn't ask for some of my past to resurface, but what I do know, is it had been healing. Finding an ideal mate, I did get everything I wanted at the time. I was looking for a protector, someone whose parents were together, someone who was affectionate even though I wasn't. Someone who wasn't an alcoholic or didn't have a drug addiction, someone who honored their mother because I figured they would treat their wife the same way. I wanted someone

Life in the Jetstream

with a great work ethic, sense of humor and most of all, I didn't want a playboy. I was tired of the run around, the lies, and the charming demeanor with the knife going through my back.

We can't go through life worrying. Learn to communicate what you think and feel. I didn't know how to be happy. Many of our problems came because of the expectations I had about marriage or relationships. Take the focus off what you don't have and focus on what you DO have. Think about why you fell in love in the first place. If you have an excuse, accept the fact we make mistakes. Learn to honor and respect them anyway. You are the only person who can make you happy. Serious relationships you need to learn to ask the hard questions. Most of you that are having relationship problems, probably didn't go to pre-marital counseling. I didn't either. Who knew sharing one life together could be so difficult yet so wonderful. People change, and relationships change. We evolve into the people we want to become. The idea is to grow together.

Chapter 9

(Layovers)
Let the Adventures Begin

MY JOB AS A FLIGHT ATTENDANT HAS ALLOWED ME TO SEE THE WORLD and take my family along for the ride. I often get asked what my favorite city to fly to is. I have been all over the globe and still have many destinations I haven't ventured to yet. I have been to South America, Asia, Africa, the Middle East, and Europe. I wanted to highlight a few of my favorite destinations and what I like about each of them. I wished everyone had the opportunity to walk in my shoes and travel the world.

I was fortunate to live in London for three and a half years. I still love the city, but I enjoy the theatre most of all. When I moved there I often thought that only the wealthy enjoyed culture like the theatre and the arts. That is not true. London gives off a vibrant feeling, with beautiful architecture and lots of history.

It was also a surreal experience to walk the Great Wall of China several times. It was even more amazing to loge down to the bottom of the wall after reflecting on this incredible wonder of the world. When you understand the history and the years families put into building the wall to prepare for war, you soon realize the sacrifice made was through generations of their life's work. The war never came, but many lost their lives. It was their destiny and an honor to serve. I can't imagine a place and time when your life's mission has to be what some else tells you it is. You have no idea how much we take for granted of our freedoms in America, and we have NO excuse to live a life enslaved to jobs, debt, and people.

The extent of my travels is absolutely mind-blowing. I have been so blessed to do what I've always dreamed about. There are many times I forget about the ah ha moments when I go into a city for the first time and see all the differences. My original dream was to go to Los Angeles, Paris and London. I've been to Paris numerous times, it is still breathtaking. The Eiffel Tower had been blinking since the Millennium. It shines every hour from dusk until about 1 a.m. for 10 minutes. Every now and then it's great to get a chocolate crêpe and hot chocolate, and then sit on the balcony of the museum. There is something MAGICAL about it. Paris is a city that offers so much culture. You have the Louvre, which has the Mona Lisa and the Michelangelo sculptures. Seeing the Arc de Triomphe, the

Greek district, and Sacré-Coeur, is something everyone should do at least once in their lives.

You can walk for hours and not see everything. Notre Dame is a masterpiece. It's located by the Seine River and adjacent to the Latin Quarters. I'd frequent those restaurants often. You have the quaint cobblestone streets, and the Greek restaurants where you can break plates on the floor and dance on the tables. It's such a pleasurable experience to break a few plates and dance on the table until you get the bill. The Latin Quarters have multiple restaurants, piano bars, theatres and café to choose from.

The next few stories will highlight what can happen and what is happening all over the world. Several adventures of mine are made-for-TV movies, but I think this one takes the cake. I'm going to invite you on a journey with me through some of my adventures and some of my nightmares. I could have easily been a reporter broadcasting these events all over the world. I look at things differently, having taken part in so many events that you only read about or see on television.

Held Hostage in Beijing

I was flying Purser to Beijing in 2009. The Purser is the

person who is in charge of the crew, delegating responsibility and making sure there is proper flow in the flight. Many of the crews love flying to Beijing, so when the flight lands, we hit the ground running. Shop! Shop! Shop! It is finally a place that is affordable to have clothes tailor made, be pampered at the spa, buy inexpensive jewelry, and also purchase gifts galore.

I arrived at the hotel and my tailor was already there. She came to my room, fitting the outfits I had that needed altering, including my uniform. My first stop was to Taipan. This is a sheik spa where I always order the foot massage. It's an hour and a half of massaging from head to toe. Don't ask me why they call it a foot massage. They offer us food and beverages, most of which are on the house. If not, it only costs a dollar or two. The lights are dim and the music is soft. A lot of us tend to fall asleep after a 14-hour flight. We are basically getting our bodies ready for an all-out sprint.

The next place we are headed to is the famous Silk market. I went to Marie's beads where she sells pearls, Swarovski crystals and Murano glass shaped in many colors and sizes. This is a women's haven. Jewels everywhere you look, so many that it's hard to fathom. At

Chapter 9

Marie's, I try to pick up the breast cancer pink glass necklaces for fundraising or even donating to survivors. I liked to get the yellow glass ribbons to support the soldiers. There is so much to choose from, but I pick something up here on most occasions. I would go to my other usual stops before calling it a night.

I headed back to the hotel, which is a five-star hotel with wonderful beds. When you stay in as many hotels that we do there is a certain expectation. As Purser, I was allowed to go have drinks and appetizers with dinner in the VIP lounge where breakfast was served every morning. It was on the top floor with a stunning view of Beijing. We were next door to the Ritz-Carlton. After appetizers, I stopped by the business center to check the computer. I had ordered an in-room massage for the first time. I would have had waxing, manicure and pedicures done. I was at the new hotel, so I was going to try out the massages. You have heard the saying "Champagne taste on a beer budget." Well, I treated myself like a QUEEN in China.

It all seemed so pleasant and relaxing from the night before. I met one of my colleagues downstairs after breakfast to go to the Pearl Market. We decided to check out the handbags, belts, clothing, and wallets behind the

169

Pearl market in another building. It is a place we normally go to and have done business there many times. I never thought anything about it. Its location was a bit obscure, going down back alleys through what looked like apartment buildings. The building we were in was NOT a storefront. However, many vendors were selling out of most of the rooms, but you have to be invited in. There are little cameras watching to see who is at the door. I guess that was a bit strange. I thought it was a cultural thing.

Anne and I arrived at the shop bright and early. It was around 9 a.m. While we were in the store shopping, we had three Chicago crew members come in the shop a bit frantically, telling the owner that two men were beating up the girl next door. What I didn't know at the time was the girl next door worked for Li, the owner also. The crew members were telling her to call the police, and with uncertainty, she finally did.

What we didn't know was the trouble that was going to follow. When the police arrived, we were in the store that had four rooms. Two were like secret smaller rooms. They made us go to the back room and sit down on the floor. The workers turned off all the surveillance machines, lights went off, air condition went off, and the door closed in

Chapter 9

behind us. Five of us were sitting on the floor in the furthest room while Li's workers were manning the second door. At first it was kind of amusing being put in that position. We didn't actually know what was going on. After a few hours we were hot, tired of sitting there, wondering what was happening and WHO we were really hiding from. I originally thought that if the men who had beat up the girl next door saw us, they would come after us too, so that's why I stayed. It became much more apparent later that we weren't hiding from them.

We were on the floor trying to make an exit plan. We were being told it should be over soon. We asked, "What is the problem here?" It was unveiled that we were being held hostage. We speculated this entire time when we were alone. All of the sudden, a cell phone rang in the store, and we all gasped, wondering why the girl who worked there would allow the phone to ring if we were in hiding. The Chicago flight attendant yelled, "Can't you turn that bleeping thing off?" I knew we were in a bad situation, but we still didn't understand the severity of it.

The owner of the store we were in also owned the store next door. She had to call her husband in to assist. It is very corrupt over there and many of the tenants were NOT

171

supposed to be selling there. After the police dealt with the assault case, they began to raid the building. We started stuffing money in our bras, and credit cards in our shoes. The other crew started getting angry and wanted to leave. You could cut the tension with a knife. I asked them, "What is the worst thing that could happen?" We had no idea what the consequences would be if we tried to walk out, especially after hiding the entire time. I've seen the shows where the police can arrest you for anything or take what you have in your possession.

We were about to hit three hours of sitting on the ground wondering what our fate held. Finally, the girl who worked there said it would only be a few more minutes and the boss was paying off the police. When Li walked into the shop, she acted as if nothing were wrong and that we should continue shopping. We were livid. All the other girls picked up a purse and said they were taking it for their trouble, but I asked for a purse and got NOTHING! I had spent a lot of money with her in the past. I was also the only one buying something that day. A FREE purse for four of the others and I got the shaft. I was very disappointed to say the least. Needless to say, that was my last visit there.

Chapter 9

We had been frantic about missing our flight. We were worried if we would go to jail or get our money taken. We were sweating, sitting on concrete for three hours, just trying to make sense of the situation. It was finally over. We could leave. Anne decided she'd had enough and was heading back to the hotel. The Chicago crew did the same. I don't get to China often, so I decided to keep moving. I needed to pick up a scarf and some make-up. I caught a cab to the next wholesale market by myself. I got there and took a look around as if I had never been to this market.

I met a wonderful local girl who was helping me with translation. I bought a few packaging items there and decided to go back to the hotel. I needed to rush to get dressed for work for my flight home. I went out to hail a cab back to the hotel and stood for just over an hour trying to get a taxi. It was during the 5 o'clock shift change, and no taxi wanted to drive me that far. I was approached by a couple of men who offered me a ride in their car for a higher price than a taxi. My options were limited, so the local girl said she would go with me if I just paid her cab fare. That was helpful because I didn't speak the language.

After that morning's experience, I said to myself, what luck! I was worried about getting in the car with anyone other than a taxi because I was aware of human trafficking that was and is still prevalent. Especially as a green-eyed Western woman with long blonde hair which was in high demand. It would be a sad conversation telling my children that; Mommy was snatched and sold because she wanted to go shopping by herself after already experiencing a major catastrophe earlier. I am no doubt an adventurer and a free spirit. I wait for no one and forge my way whenever possible. However, I attempt to think logically most of the time. It was no wonder I was put in so many bad situations.

We made it back to the hotel in one piece. I had no time to spare. I needed to jet across the street to give a friend items I couldn't carry with me. I didn't realize I was at my duty-free limit. I was running as fast as I could and was drenched in sweat. I ran to the hotel lobby and asked if my uniform been delivered yet. The answer was NO. I was absolutely beside myself. I went upstairs to call my tailor because I did not have another uniform to wear home. She wasn't there, so I jumped in the shower and then finished packing. About three minutes before I was supposed to get picked up, she arrived with my dress. I was in a frenzy trying to get downstairs. I made it on the bus and took the biggest sigh of relief I could. I was so happy to have a break to get some rest.

Chapter 9

We arrived at the airport, boarded our flight, and we had a delay. My goodness, was this going to ever end? I won't bore you with the details, but we eventually made it to DC. I had to commute on an hour flight and then drive another hour. This is normally my wind-down time before I walk in the door to announce, "Honey and boys, I'm home," as if NOTHING ever happened. The humorous thing about this, I was talking to my friend Jen about the so-called adventure. She and her husband pitch TV shows in LA.

She was giving me a play-by-play on how well the story would play out on screen. She said, "The camera watches you drive up to your suburban ranch home. You get out of the car and your family welcomes you at the door with smiles, kisses and hugs. As you are walking into the living room to see how their weekend was, your dress tears at the pocket. You just smile looking into the camera as if you knew what went on and shake it off without speaking of the trip to the family." It was hysterical when she was saying that, because I hadn't told her that my uniform was at the tailor. I was moving buttons, adding a zipper, and closing up my pockets. The dress arrived just in the nick of time as I was meeting the crew for pick-up. The story was written for a movie as if I were an undercover agent. It was definitely a trip to remember. We laugh about it now, but

I'm fully aware of the danger I put myself in that weekend.

Catastrophic Events

Earthquakes

I had only been a flight attendant for a few years. I was on a layover at the Hilton on Century Boulevard in Los Angeles on June 28, 1992. Earlier that day, I was at the pool. I met some people and had a pleasant day. That night was not unusual; I ate dinner, watched some television, and went to bed. I woke up to lights flickering, the hotel swaying, pictures falling and drawers opening. I was on the 8th floor. I couldn't even get out of bed, I was so frightened. I didn't know what was happening at first. This had to be an earthquake. I dialed my mom's number in the dark for a familiar voice. What's comical about this for me is I had to use the calling cards with those long numbers to make the call. I had it memorized. I dialed and told her I was in the middle of an earthquake and that I was fine but shaken. I wanted her to tell me what to do. I had heard not to run down the stairs, that it was best to stand in the doorway.

I had another little problem. I used to sleep without pajamas on, so I was scurrying around the dark to find clothes to put on. Then I could at least look out my door to see what everyone else was doing. I finally put some

Chapter 9

clothes on and my mom helped calm me down from not knowing what to do. When I got off the phone, a friend I met earlier at the pool called to see if I was okay. After things settled down, we got together to talk about it.

When my girlfriend, Jen moved to LA, we were living in Hollywood Hills at the time. We lived near the Hollywood sign on Beachwood Drive. She and I had been out that day and we were driving by the Viper Room discussing River Phoenix's death, as we drove by, the radio hosts were talking about an earthquake. We had been preoccupied by what we were chatting about, so we didn't understand what they were really saying. We only heard the word "earthquake," so we kind of laughed it off as if they were talking about something that already happened. It was January 1994.

We went to bed; we were awakened at about 5:32 a.m. by a rumbling sound. It was another earthquake for me and the first for her. Once again, I was scared stiff and couldn't move. I yelled out to her to come to my room while she yelled for me to go there, so I jumped up and ran in there. Once again, I didn't know what to do, but because the houses have been there for so many years, I didn't know what could happen. We both threw on some sweats and a t-shirt and ran outside. The house we lived in weathered well. A few others were brought to the ground. It was heartbreaking.

Just in the past few years, you have heard about all the earthquakes going on in Japan and the continuing aftershocks. On our layovers, we run into serious catastrophes that Mother Nature puts in our way. We had to get a little smarter when things happened. Learn how to stay safe, if at all possible. When I flew to Japan immediately after one of the quakes, I can't say I wasn't cautious. I found my nearest exits, which you should do anyway. I also brought extra food and water in case there wasn't any available. Don't take the elevators and stay calm. The doorway is the strongest place to take cover. I was told not to put my double lock on the door, because when the hotel shifts it may keep me locked in there for who knows how long. Fortunately, that layover was smooth sailing.

Mudslides, Bombings and Riots

I have seen the devastation of mudslides in Caracas, Venezuela in 1999. It ate up the town where we once stayed on the beach, and soon after the city became a crime-infested area. We'd fly to Lima, Peru where the

Chapter 9

police stand in front of banks with AK-47s. Guerrilla warfare is still alive and happening today. I was in LA at the Hilton during the lock down after Rodney King was beaten. People were protesting in the streets; there were fires and looting again. We had put on clothes to hit the town, but found out we were unable to leave the hotel. I sat with another crew member saying, "We're all dressed up with nowhere to go." I have the picture of us together to commemorate that night. It was April of 1992. Who would ever think you could get arrested for leaving your hotel? I'd rather be safe anyway. You may remember the riots in Bahrain in 2013. I was there for that but stayed in the hotel the first trip and had to stay on the plane the next trip.

When I lived in London, there were several car bombs that went off, but somehow it didn't seem to faze me. Not until I was able to see the destruction for myself, the people affected by it and the memorials. Some years ago there were several bombs that went off at different underground stations in London. Our hotel was beside the Edgeware Station stop. I arrived the day after the bomb went off on July 7, 2005. It was still chaotic; people were bringing flowers and crying hysterically. Our hotel was a triage center. It makes it very real when you are witness to the tragic event while it's happening. It's easy to disregard it when you watch the news thousands of miles away without a care in the world.

I don't always choose my words carefully, but after experiencing so many tragic events that truly are devastating, you know how NOT to use them. I do my best not to use those words to describe daily or weekly activities. Breaking a nail, dropping the groceries, losing the keys, forgetting my checkbook, or whatever it may be, we can get over that. People all over the world suffer political, racial, and economic crisis that we can't even imagine. There are things I know I couldn't even talk about from the countries I travel to, in fear of what might happen. Recently, there was an argument with people complaining about America. An acquaintance I know from Syria stepped up and said, "Are your people decapitating others on a daily basis?" That certainly puts things in perspective. Doesn't it? I'm grateful to have the freedom of speech in my country. In several countries I fly to, you can't watch certain shows, videos, or even get on social media. We have places where alcohol is illegal and places where you can't talk about democracy.

I can tell you, I had a great time seeing Russia. There are some amazing places to see, which I may have talked about already, but there were a small amount of things I found dated and odd. When we'd leave our hotel in Russia, we had to carry our passport and a form stating where we were staying. You have cultural differences everywhere you go, so I thought I'd just be going through the motions by doing this. I was walking back toward the hotel, coming from behind the Kremlin where there was a walk way. We were just having a hard time figuring out which way to go. I saw police everywhere throughout Russia, but it just never sunk in. I had watched them ask for papers the week before when I saw the guy get taken away. Well, what do you think I want to do when I see one of those guys now? I was to avoid them if at all possible. We rounded the corner and continued to walk. We could go one of two ways to get back to the hotel. We were walking on the path all tourists take by the Kremlin. I saw officers and we decided to head for the bridge to cross the street.

One of the officers called us to come over to them. I'm pointing at myself saying, "Me! Are you calling me?" I don't speak the language, so that makes it harder to communicate. Yes, it was me they wanted. Another crew member and I walked over to the two men. I don't know how much you know about Russians, but they do not have the friendly faces and the customer service skills that we appreciate in the states. They look mad as if you did something wrong. He asked for my papers and the only way I knew that was because he pointed at me and swung a paper in his hand. At first I'm like, "What?" I'd never been asked before, so I handed him my passport and papers.

Every scenario was running through my brain. Was I in trouble? Were they going to take me somewhere? I didn't speak the language. Who would I call? Would I even get a call? He tried asking me questions that I didn't understand. After a few questions, he gave up and sent me on my way. I was relieved. Of course, I had to ask the staff at the hotel, why they do that? What are they looking for? I stayed close to hotel if I was hungry. We never could figure out the reasoning behind checking our papers.

Buenos Aires Political & Economic Collapse

I also remember being in Buenos Aires during the political and economic collapse. It was my birthday, December 19, 2001. I was in Puerto Madero, standing on the rooftop of my hotel and watching the fires break out around the city. We saw the helicopter fly in to pick up the President, Fernando de la Rua. There was rioting, looting, and people running to the banks only to find they were closed. The police were shooting in all directions. I was getting edgy, wondering if we would make it out of there. Would we be able to fly home where we're safe? You feel protected in a five-star hotel with all the comforts and conveniences of home, but it really was a WAR going on out there. The country was falling apart right before my eyes. This was monumental.

My next trip to Argentina was about four days later. It reminded me of what I thought the "Depression" would look like. I had never seen so many people lining up and surrounding the banks. Their money had devalued significantly. People were unable to get their money from the banks. The desperation on the people's faces is imbedded in my mind. I went out to get food and was able to see the destruction around town. I even had flying partners being robbed while getting in and out of cabs going to get food for their layovers.

I had heard the stories years before when companies and personal properties were seized illegally by the government without notice. Some of our friends from Palm Beach were from Argentina. Our son's martial arts teacher was one of them. I met his parents who still lived in the city, and they told me about what happened to them. They worked their entire lives and everything was taken. They had to start over. They were lovely people. They were well-dressed, well-spoken, and resilient. They didn't complain, make excuses, or hold anyone accountable.

Can you imagine working your entire life for something and having it taken away in an instant? Today in the U.S., it's happening with job losses, downsizing, the real estate market, and other avenues. My question for you is if everything you had taken away tomorrow, how would you feel about starting over? I can tell you from my experience, most can't handle daily inconveniences, let alone starting over. It's a reality check to think about what's going on around the world, but we don't think it could happen to us.

I always loved going to Buenos Aires, Argentina, where our money goes a long way. The beef there is unlike any other you will find in the world. It melts in your mouth. You can enjoy a six-course meal for about $30 and that includes wine. We stayed in Puerto Madero on the water. A must-see is a tango show. You have a few good ones to choose from. There is Señor Tango and La Ventana. I suggest taking the city bus to see the many highlights of the area. You'll go through Palermo, Rigoletta, La Boca, and many other places. Lots of people want to see where Evita "Eva Peron" is buried.

Chapter 9

Oktoberfest

We can go to the other side of the world in Europe. I had the opportunity to go to the infamous Oktoberfest on four occasions. The first time, I went with the crew at 9:30 in the morning. We were told if we didn't show up early, we wouldn't get a seat. There are sometimes up to 10,000 people per tent. This was my introduction. The following year, I brought my husband because I know it was more of his speed than mine. I loved the music and bands playing. I enjoyed the atmosphere because everyone is happy and you don't meet a stranger. We arrived at the Paulaner tent with the crew soon after we landed in Munich. We couldn't believe how big the beers were and how many these women could carry. The pretzels were as big as our faces. Everything was just HUGE!

We were probably only there for about three hours. We all were laughing, joking, and taking photos. We were making friends with people from the other tables. People come from all over the world. My husband was constantly the life of the party. It was no different in Germany. He made his mark. I was just starting on my second beer when Karen, one of the crew members, went with me to the bathroom. After washing our hands, I stepped back to look in the mirror and put on some lip gloss. The girl in front of me bent over and flipped her long hair back. Her head made contact with my temple and I lost my balance.

I grabbed my head in disbelief. It was painful. Did that just happen? Karen and I walked back to our table and the action was in full swing. We were trying to tell my husband what happened in the bathroom and it sounded a bit unreal even to me. I started getting a migraine headache and slowly blacking out. It was time to leave. I had no idea how to get back to the hotel and neither did my husband. We were totally dependent on Karen. Rob was in an unfamiliar place and had a little too much to drink. It seemed as if I did too, but I knew I hadn't. Karen had to guide me and hold me up as my coordination disappeared. I continued to fade in and out on our way back to the hotel. Finally, we made it back and Karen thought it would be good for us to have some food, so she got us to the room and then went back out for sandwiches. I tried to eat when she came back, but it just made me more nauseous.

I tried sleeping, hoping that would help, but I had the worst migraine I'd ever had in my life. I ran a hot bath thinking that would make a difference. I practically filled it up three times and stayed there throughout the night. I was so sick and my head hurt so bad, I wished the flight would have been cancelled. That didn't happen. I ended up working back to DC just so I could get home and rest. I headed to the doctor to find out I had a concussion. After this incident, I had no intentions of ever going back to another Oktoberfest again. It certainly put a bad taste in my mouth.

A few years later my husband's old police partner wanted to go to Munich to visit the BMW factory and go to Oktoberfest. I told my husband to go with him. If I got the trip, we'd go together. My husband and I love theme parties. So he talked me into going so we could wear our Lederhosen and Drundel. It was a different experience this time. I didn't have anything to drink, enjoyed dressing up and stayed away from girls flipping their hair. Rob and Ed had a great time together. I have to say that everyone should go to Oktoberfest at least once.

I enjoyed going whitewater rafting in Maipo Valley, Chile. The water was absolutely freezing and about 12 of us ventured down the river expecting the unexpected. I also flew Copenhagen, Denmark for a few months. It was a quaint, hospitable city. It was around the holidays with a city made of an ice sculpture, a skating rink, a laser show; train's to take you around the park, a gnome's home as well as many café, and shops to buy your wares. During the first visit, I was with a flying partner who had a friend from Denmark meeting up with her on the layover. She asked if we wanted to join her for some sightseeing. Of course we did. You never know where you will end up when sightseeing. We ended up driving to Sweden for dinner. It was wonderful. That was a unique and memorable experience.

I won an eight-day cruise with a nutritional company back in 1998. This was a first for me. I had such an awesome time getting to know the movers and shakers of the company. We all bonded and started venturing out together. The highlights of the trip were the toga party by the pool and cave tubing in Belize. We rented a jeep and drove around Grand Cayman Island to the Seven Mile Beach. When we got to Belize, we decided to go cave tubing. We hiked up the mountain and rode the tubes coming down with the lights on our heads. Bats were flying around. We made a chain, everyone holding on to something of each other's: a tube, a hand, or a foot, so we wouldn't get separated.

We did this on our own, not with the cruise line, so we were getting behind on time. It took about an hour to get

Chapter 9

there, so we were hoping and praying we'd made it back in time to catch the ship. Once again, in the nick of time, we barely made it back because the cab driver called security saying we didn't pay him enough. It was like the Amazing Race to get back. We all had different transportation rushing back to see who actually made it to check-in. There were five of us catching the LAST little boat back to the ship; thankfully, we didn't get left behind.

I had won another trip to Panama Canal, which was quite interesting. It is not a destination I would have selected, but it made for an unbelievable vacation. There were others who qualified for the trip, and we all were treated like VIPs. We had the Survivor tour. All of us took a boat through a swampy-looking area in the dark, hiked up a hill for the reveal of bon fires and a lavish spread of GREAT food. We took an old glass train through the forest and watched how the canal let the boats through that part. We were in the skybox where we had cocktails and watched how this happened. It's astonishing to see how much water shifts to bring the boats down to allow them to enter the next section. Definitely an art!

We came home to gifts every night on our bed. I absolutely love surprises like that. NO matter how BIG or

189

small, a gesture of kindness goes a long way in my book. The next morning, we were off to our own private island. There was food, horseback riding, canoeing, snorkeling, lying in hammocks, sunbathing, or whatever our hearts desired. My husband was with me trying the canoe thing. Boy, it was bad. He was over 240 lbs. and I wasn't light either. We kept tipping the boat over. It became a lost cause in the end. We went snorkeling with everyone else instead. I enjoyed doing that.

One of the girls hit a reef and her body was bright red all over. She was hurting and in a lot of pain. I didn't think anything of it until I was stuck between two reefs pretty far out. I started to hyperventilate, so I swam to my husband to get me back to the dock on the island. He took me around the reef and headed back out with the others. At that point the island was my friend. I went horseback riding and lay in the hammock for some sun. Tranquil and peaceful!

I went on a cruise with my family in 2009. This was their first cruise. We decided to kill two birds with one stone. See our friends in LA and take the cruise from there to Baja, Cabo San Lucas, Puerto Vallarta, and Mazatlan. We spent the first two days on our friend's house-boat in Marina Del Rey. This would get all of us ready for the

Chapter 9

motion in the ocean, which I don't think is that bad anyway. We had season tickets for Magic Mountain and headed there for a day of adventure. We had some of our friends meet us at the boat and had dinner. Then off we went to the cruise.

My sons loved the freedom it allowed. They could be mobile and make friends. Royal Caribbean's ship was spectacular. They had an ice skating rink, rock climbing, miniature golf, a skating park, kids' hang outs, a cool promenade, game rooms, a few pools, and so much more. I was going to enjoy some sun and shows. I rave about the five- star restaurants where we had the opportunity to DRESS UP! Yes, I still like to play dress-up.

My family opted to go on our own and take a cab to the beach. We bought a cabana and a bucket of drinks. Then we saw people parasailing. How cool is that? My husband said he wanted to go and it was his 35th birthday. He always told me not to do anything like that and now he wanted to go. I checked out the price, and he and my oldest son, Austin, decided to go. My youngest son, Kieran, and I watched them high in the sky. I thought: it's not that bad, I guess. It was an unforgettable experience for them both. Kieran then decided he wanted to go. He was nine years old.

Should you let a nine-year-old do something like that? I consulted with my husband and he agreed, so there went Kieran parasailing.

I thought to myself: what kind of mother are you? You would never forgive yourself if something happened. I decided to go ahead and take the plunge and try it myself. I took off and realized I was not in the seat properly. I was petrified because looking up it doesn't seem so high, but looking down, I thought I would die. It was finally time for me to come down, not a moment too soon for me. However, I had trouble pulling hard enough to stop on the target and ended up partially in the water. I'm glad I did it once, but I can assure you, you won't see me in ANY lines trying that again.

Stalked in Sao Paulo, Brazil

One of my least favorite destinations during my travel experiences was Sao Paulo, Brazil. I want to show you how things change and how life unfolds sometimes when we don't even realize it. My first trip to Brazil set the stage for the ones to come. I was living in London and flew through Miami to Sao Paulo in 1992. I was thrilled to see a new country. We started off doing some sightseeing downtown during the day. I remember photographing the shacks

Chapter 9

people were living in and the garbage piled up on the roads. Not quite what I was expecting.

The crew decided to go out that night and see the nightlife. We headed to the Limelight to dance. We had a great time. I ending up dancing with the guy doing the show that night called the "Brazilian Michael Jackson." It was a lot of fun. He didn't speak English and I didn't speak Portuguese. I had two of the Portuguese speakers on the crew, Chris and Ana, with me. They did the little translation I needed that night.

The next day, one of my crew members, Kerry, and I were going to get a bite to eat for lunch. Well I had a surprise visitor from last night. The Brazilian Michael Jackson showed up and wanted to talk. HOW? He didn't speak English. The other thing was I didn't invite him to come over. I finally had to get Ana the speaker to talk to him and tell him he needed to leave; it made me uncomfortable. I was trying to walk out the front door and he kept sitting there waiting for me to come down. I thought he was gone and we came down to go to lunch and he jumped from behind the sign. I freaked out and ran back to my room.

Life in the Jetstream

Kerry F. and I decided to go down the employee elevator and go out the back entrance. The employees were telling us we couldn't be there, and I just apologized and ran out. We had lunch and returned to the hotel. I stayed back while I sent her in to see if he was gone. We ran in the hotel up the elevator to my room. I made it. The next thing I know, the hotel desk was calling me and said I had a message they needed to deliver. They knocked on the door and delivered a note and a dozen roses. The gesture was nice, but the fact that this guy showed up without my knowledge made it difficult for me to trust him.

During my next several trips to Brazil, I encountered a guy on my way to the grocery store who decided to streak. He had a long coat on with NOTHING on underneath. That's something you run from. We had crew members robbed at gunpoint. It was not safe to go out at night or even in the day if you are alone. It makes it difficult when you need to find food on your layovers. It put a bad taste in my mouth.

I have spent many years going to Brazil, and it wasn't all bad. Within the past couple of years, another transition with our company took place. I'm doing what I absolutely love, but it has changed. I have 25 years seniority and I've found myself sitting on reserve. This means I'm on call and the company decides where I'll fly to. I spend a lot of time in the airport waiting. It gives me time to think about even the places I didn't enjoy going to. When we start this job, we are anxious to see everything. After years of flying, we decide which places we like or don't like, where we will or won't go. We are able to choose. When that gets taken a way, it turns our world upside down. It affects our schedule, the amount of money we make, and places we can no longer go.

Riots & Protesting the Economics of World Cup and Olympics

I headed back to Brazil where the riots have started because of the money spent for the World Cup and the Olympics. The Brazilians believe the money should go towards education. Billions of dollars were given to Brazil to support efforts to rebuild and make it worthy for the International Games. Unfortunately, the progress has been slow and not enough changes are being made to support the amount of money given. I can personally see the oversized walls on the road sides that hide the poverty and trash behind them. It reminds me of China when they were getting ready for the Olympics. It was all smoke and mirrors. They landscaped beautifully everywhere, even on the roadside. They moved the people out of their dilapidated living conditions to beautify the area, not knowing if they had anywhere else to go. They shut the factories down for two weeks so there wasn't as much pollution in the air when tourists arrived. The prices went up for supply and demand and never seemed to come down after that. I support the Games; however, if you look deeper at who's paying the real price, you'd be surprised. We can say that's a huge amount of money to build or restructure a city, but think about where the money really goes.

It changed my perspective. I can see how I was saying, "I can't stand going to THAT place." Yet today, I'm so fortunate to go to any of these places. Brazil looks good now. We have to look at the positive we can bring from every situation instead of focusing on everything that's wrong with it. It took me a long time to grasp this, so I believe I had to go through it to truly understand it.

I'm heading to Rio de Janeiro. I used to talk about the downside of Rio, like the crime, poverty, the infrastructure, and other shortcomings. Now, I see the beautiful water, the mountainous landscape, and Corcovado, the Christ statue we pass every time I'm in the country. It's amazing! Just as

Chapter 9

people talk about the negatives, it's just as easy to see the bright side.

Ask Yourself:

Have you ever wanted to travel? Where do you want to go? What kind of activities do you want to participate in? Did you want to learn another language? What adventures have you been through that put a smile on your face today? Where's your bucket list?

Life's Lessons:

I decided to take advantage of all the traveling opportunities I had. We are not promised tomorrow. About 12 years ago, when my airline went bankrupt, I thought it was over. I didn't want to waste the time I had. Every city and country has something to offer. Don't wait to do the things you really want to do. My husband's father waited for years to retire and fish. He became disabled, and today he can't even drive. He never leaves the home except to go to the doctors. His advice would be to enjoy life every day.

We can choose to live on autopilot or go full throttle. Don't look back with regret. Make your bucket list of places to go. Be adventurous! My husband and I have a new goal to visit ALL of the Wonders of the World. We have seen quite a few and some of the others may have to wait because of the political unrest in those areas. However, we have a plan and are taking the steps to accomplish each goal. I hope you will join us and do the same.

Chapter 10

(Balancing the Cargo)
Weighing Your Options

I WAS ALWAYS A BIT HEAVY GROWING UP. I remember being made fun of more often than not. I tried to make a conscience effort to hold my stomach in as a child. When we moved to Virginia and got a place of our own, I was walking down the hallway and my brother said something to me about being fat. I lifted up my shirt to see my stomach and I got excited. I was skinny! Wow! How did I miss getting skinny? I guess after getting taller and older, I lost the baby fat. I was about 11 years old then. This shows how the mind is a powerful thing. What you think is what you are.

Weight is that nasty subject I know most women want to avoid. Women think it's a constant reminder of how inadequate we are. I have worked with and talked to so many people who were fighting the battle of the bulge. I am an average person when it comes to being healthy and looking the part. While pregnant with my first child, I gained more than 70 lbs., tipping the scale at just over 200 lbs. I let this be a crutch for me for many years. I would try to convince myself that I'm married and my husband should love me unconditionally anyway. I know you've said it too, so let me have my excuses. I enjoy my comfort food. I would always say, "There are few things left in life to enjoy, so why can't food be one of them?"

I was steadily gaining weight over the years. We had owned two gyms and I absolutely hated to workout. I did initially drop 12 pounds and we did believe in supplementation. Our soil is depleted of vitamins and minerals. There is also more toxicity in the air, the food, and the water supply. Our bodies are their own miracles, if we treat them right. Unfortunately, we don't create those vitamins and minerals in our body so we have to get them from somewhere. It doesn't matter if you are eating 100% organic; you are still lacking.

We have to remember that a pill will never be the end all form to lose weight or get healthy. We look for the easy way out. I've tried many diets and weight loss pills over the years. Guess what? I found there was NO easy way. Simpler ways, YES! Ask anyone who has been on yo-yo diets for years. What works for you may not for me. We think cheap and easy is the answer to everything.

Chapter 10

My husband has always enjoyed the process of staying fit and healthy. He eventually became a personal trainer and works out much of the time. However, his nutrition needed some help. I have become much more interested in my health today. We don't realize how many medications are causing multiple side effects attributing to disease, even obesity. Watch any TV advertisement on ANY medicine. Let's take for instance anti-depressants. As you read the super fine print, you'll see that the pills may cause nausea, vomiting, diarrhea, bloating, sharp abdominal pains, and suicidal tendencies. Knowing this can happen, WHY do we take them? These are the reasons I use medication as a LAST resort.

My father was on 18 medications a day. Okay, 16 every day and two additional in the same week. He had already had two heart attacks in the past, had high blood pressure and high cholesterol, among other things. Let me say this, I'm NOT a doctor. I am grateful for doctors because we need them. I'm just hoping more people will educate themselves, be pro-active, and take the holistic approach first. Most medications are Band-Aids, not cures.

The reason I feel so strongly about this is because my father is no longer here to talk about it. He took his own life in the driveway of my family home. My nephew and sons were in the car nearby, getting ready to go to church. The sound will resonate with those children for the rest of their lives. My brother watched helplessly. Not a moment to speak, in the blink of an eye, there was NOTHING my brother could do to stop the fatal shot.

I was in London, England, at the time. I woke up to a call at 3:45 a.m. and was told there had been an "accident." I wasn't told anything else. My mind was racing because when I last spoke to my dad, he was feeding my youngest son, Kieran. I packed and left for Heathrow as quickly as possible to get on the first flight back. My aunt and uncle picked me up from the airport and we were waiting for my husband to fly in from Florida. He had just gotten to our Palm Beach home after flying back from London a day earlier.

As we waited, I was asking questions about what happened and they wouldn't tell me anything. I was exhausted and cried the whole way home, so I decided to lie down until my husband arrived. My parents lived about an hour from the airport so I couldn't go straight home. Finally he got to Greensboro and my uncle drove us to Martinsville. I continued to ask questions and my uncle

Chapter 10

pulled over to go into the country store so my husband could tell me the TRUTH. Rob proceeded to tell me my dad had shot himself. What?

I was left with a lot of questions and no answers. I wondered how life could get THAT bad. I did not have the best relationship with my father growing up but it didn't make ANY sense to me. I could have seen that coming if he were alone, but NOT with the kids around. However, one thing I knew for sure was his grandchildren were the ONLY unconditional love my father had ever known. He lit up when they were around.

It has taken years for me to process what happened. My family still feels the effects of that day. I had buried the memories of the past, which kept me from having a good relationship with my dad. Bad things happen to people, but it is how we react that will shape our character. We should draw strength and courage in our darkest hours. God always has a plan for us, even when we can't see it ourselves.

That was a tragic experience we had to go through. I do believe in my heart that multiple medications and the resulting side effects contributed to what ultimately happened. There is no turning back. I ask everyone taking medications to be diligent, to educate themselves, and to write down the side effects to be aware. Knowledge is power. We rely on doctors and their expertise, but in the end it's still called a "PRACTICE." You have heard them say, "Try this, if it doesn't work we will try something else. "WHY are we OK with that, in most cases?" Start understanding the benefits of natural remedies. Ask questions and ask if there are personal changes you can make before immediately taking something new.

If you've noticed, many become a product of our environment. How many people in Hollywood are obese? You are probably saying it's because they have to stay fit for their job. Look at places like Denver, Miami and New York City. They realize the importance of being healthy. They have access to more options. Guess what? Technology today allows us to reach anywhere in the world at any time. We might not be able to pick it up today, but we can have anything we want. When I am talking about being healthy, it has nothing to do with being heavy or skinny. There are many unhealthy skinny people, so don't compare yourself.

I have been great at the excuses for not losing weight. I

Chapter 10

travel so much, there are so many preservatives in the food, healthy food costs too much, and we don't have many organic foods locally, and so forth. BLAH, BLAH, BLAH! Do you know the definition of an "EXCUSE?" The definition is a well-planned lie as my mentor, Dani would state. When does enough become enough? I cringe when people say I NEED to drop the weight, but WE DON'T Why? We don't want to give up ANYTHING! It's too hard, my health is fine right now, and we are comfortable to stay that way. Let me say this. We ALL pay the price! You just have to ask yourself, do you want to pay NOW or LATER? Ultimately, you will PAY the price. Why do we wait till our health is deteriorating to realize we need to do something different?

I get asked all of the time, "How can you keep the weight off?" People also say, "I want to lose it all this month." It took you longer to put it on than thirty days, so give it time. Losing weight is a state of mind. Change your way of thinking. My first ah- ha moment came when I was in Brazil, having breakfast with a flying partner, Stacey. She was just starting her body-building career and looked phenomenal. This was March of 2010. I certainly wanted what she was having. I watched her eat and was shocked at how much food she was consuming. With most diets, you can't have a lot of food or you're counting points or calories. You think you are going to die(t) because you are going without, which makes you crave many things.

After Stacey told me you could eat all you want, I was like, "Yeah, I'm all in." There was a catch. To speed up your metabolism you need to eat five or six small meals a day. Sounds like a plan to me. She told me to buy a book about Eating Clean. It is NOT a diet. I know; I was carrying around The 4 Day Diet back then. I loved The Celebrity Fit Club and The Biggest Loser. This allowed me to cater to my specific lifestyle. There were a variety of options to drop weight fast, slow, accelerated, gluten-free, or whatever your situation may be.

I have always been a picky eater. I don't like that I'm that way at all. I had to select the things I could or would eat. Most of us need incentive or motivation to lose weight. Let me give you a few ideas on what might help.

- Your future health will depend on it.

- If you have children or grandchildren, they want you around for years to come.

- Your spouse deserves to keep the person they fell in

Chapter 10

love with.

- Don't you want to FEEL and LOOK your BEST?

Remember this, 75 percent is nutrition, 15 percent is training and 10 percent is genetic. Take control of your eating habits. It's fine to cheat every now and then. What we really want to incorporate is a truly healthy lifestyle change. Don't focus on weight alone. It is how it's distributed.

I packed my food when I went overseas' and I was working out hard every chance I got. I ended up losing 25 lbs. in three months. I felt great and had a renewed zest for life. I could wear my skinny jeans again. YEAH! However, I still had some weight to lose. I had been killing myself eating super clean, carrying all my food, and working out like a maniac. Is there a better way? I was in Los Angeles on a layover and I got a call from a woman with whom I had never met. I had sent her an invitation to my "adopted" sons surprise 18th birthday party in March of 2011.

This story is a made-for-TV movie that I won't get into right now, but Ellen and Paul Ganus were on the list of guardians for Kesun at one time. They are all in the acting field. I thought this would be a great time to meet them. I had spoken to Ellen's husband, Paul, a few times on the phone, but that was the extent of it. She called to apologize for not being able to make it to the party due to a prior speaking engagement. The fortunate thing was my family wasn't able to make it either, due to load volumes being extremely high. They did not RSVP so I thought nothing of it.

When she called, she was extremely pleasant and positive. I'm drawn to people with electric personalities. During the conversation, she asked me for my e-mail, one of which was race2health. She stopped in her tracks and asked me if I was involved with health and wellness. I told her I have been involved and some of the reasons why. I told her about my dad and what drew me closer to being healthier. It was only then I found out she was a top-ranked millionaire with a leading Health and Wellness company.

We kept in touch over time and later I told her about my mission to help my community and take off my last unwanted pounds. She said why don't we do this, get 10 to 12 people together and see what the results are. I formed a test group and the outcome was astounding. My husband, being the skeptic he is, did not want to have ANYTHING to do with this. He was present the night I brought the group together. He was listening to all the questions asked and wanted to see if you truly follow the directions exactly, will it WORK? Basically, he was frustrated with all the questions everyone was asking. That's the REAL reason he tried it. He lost 15 lbs. in 10 days and 20 lbs. over the month. I lost 15 lbs. in the month. We were NOT dieting. This was the way to cleanse your body and get proper nutrition all at the same time. Finally, there's a system that works together for a healthier you.

There were a few keywords that stood out for me when Ellen and I would have a conversation. Those were, "the proof is in the results" and "the company is here to enhance your lifestyle, not stress it out." WOW! It had taken many years to get in balance and everyday I'm still learning, but that was powerful. My life is committed to helping others; however, I choose not to leave what matters most to me behind, and that's my family. I take one day at a time and the doors seem to open where I'm needed most.

Later, we were able to have the birthday party in LA for Kesun. Paul and Ellen were able to make it. It was quite laughable after returning home. When I arrived back in VA, every time I turned on the television I would see one of Paul's commercials. I told Rob he was watching to keep me on track.

What is really crazy is there are lots of people who want to see you fail when you are trying to lose weight. How sad is that? They don't want you to lose the weight or get healthy and they don't want you financially secure either. How can you say that? The more you try to achieve in life, the more resistance you encounter. People say they are happy for you, but the bottom line is that ACTIONS speak much louder than words. My advice is be bold, be unique, stop the naysayers from killing your DREAM of a better, healthier YOU, and don't go down the path of misery with them. YOU ARE GREAT! You can DO IT!

I know it's difficult, especially if you are in a town like ours setting record highs. Our town was an instant community many years ago. The factories were booming, textiles were flourishing, and people were thriving. We have lost almost all of that today, because they have moved it overseas. Martinsville statistics tops the charts with the highest teen pregnancy rates in the state of Virginia, along with the highest unemployment rate until 2013. Our poverty level is at an all- time high. What I found interesting was what makes someone come back here when the odds are against you?

Chapter 10

I do my best not to go to the doctor unless completely necessary. I ended up in the doctor's office seeing the NEW attending physician instead of my own. I had been in Ghana, Africa when I became extremely ill for several days. I had all the symptoms of malaria. During the visit, I found out the physician and I went to the same high school a few years apart. I mainly wanted to know WHY he chose to come back to Martinsville to live. He said it was the BEST place to come if you're a doctor, EVERYONE IS SICK or MEDICATED. There was no doubt in my mind that he was right. Although I was shocked he was so candid about it. The main things surviving in our town is the production industry, fast food restaurants, pharmacies, hospital, banking schools, and beauty salons.

Many years ago, I had taken a vow. I said I would NEVER come back to that town. I told you earlier that the problem with taking vows is that in most cases, the words come back to haunt you. I wanted my children to grow up around family, so we came back. I could offer the best of both worlds. We could have affordable housing, my husband could be a stay-at-home dad, which was a dream of mine, and we could fly anywhere in the world our hearts desired. Our quality of life would be immeasurable. I find my town has so much to offer. When you travel the world, I appreciate the simpler things in life. We have the Blue Ridge Mountains, Smith Mountain Lake, small town atmosphere, everything is affordable and a community of friendly people. All of us take vows and struggle to understand why we are back at square one. Choose to see the lesson in the situation. I ran from all of my problems, now I face them.

Within the next 2 years, I packed on 25 lbs. However, I was being consistent with my eating habits, but not as much with working out. In one month alone, I gained ten pounds after trying the Nuva Ring, which I had removed after 30 days. I had experienced a steady increase in weight gain immediately. What the heck? All the sudden, I started getting huge rashes and hives up and down my legs. My legs would burn after I ate certain foods. I knew there was a serious problem and I needed some help.

I finally went to an allergist and got pricked over 110 times and had eight vials of blood taken. I found out I was allergic to wheat and eggs. That's no big deal; I can go gluten-free, whatever that is. Then I was given the real news from my tests. I'm allergic to myself! How does that happen? It can sometimes lay dormant for years until it's triggered. Although I still don't fully understand it, it's an auto- immune disease. Once again, we start from scratch and eliminate things in my life that cause the problem.

I'm back religiously on the cleansing system, which I initially started. I can go gluten-free this way and reset my body to see if it's going to allow me to keep the weight off. Everything happens for a reason and I embraced the new challenge to get healthier. It's just another one of life's roadblocks. Personally, it was only sending me back to what I already knew. Consistency has not been one of my closet friends, but I believe in signs and I know to heed advice before you get hit really hard.

I also believe that our health can be tied to our unresolved issues. This can be a process. I find many emotional eaters find comfort in sweets or excessive amounts of food because of things that stem from their past. There are several great books you can read about why we eat certain things or sneak food. Who withheld food from you? Did you not have enough food? Was your daily staple sugar based foods? I encourage everyone to take it one day at a time. Choose wisely what you eat, be active, and be pro-active with your health. What I do know is if you don't have your health, your quality of life suffers.

Ask Yourself:

Have you ever struggled with your weight? Have you been on all the yo-yo diets that leave you depressed? Do you keep giving up because you don't think it's worth it? How is your weight affecting your relationships? Did you already give up?

Life's Lessons:

Weight loss is a decision you make for yourself. You cannot do it for ANYONE else, but yourself. Learn to love yourself because you are important and you do matter regardless of your size. There are many great nutritional options to help you. For me, it was important having quality products and working with others who were in the same boat, so we could cheer one another on. I was not interested in one product wonders, because everyone is quite different.

I gave up on myself many times in the past. I didn't value myself enough to believe I was worth fighting for. I am worth it and so are you. Put down the soda, chips and cheesecake. I know you're saying just one more time, I'll start tomorrow. I said the same thing. Tomorrow never comes so today is your day. My relationship was affected tremendously. I never wanted to change my clothes in front of my husband embarrassed that he wondered why I'm letting myself go. The intimacy is fleeting because of your insecurities. It's painful to face the reality of change. Make the change for yourself, when you do it for others it's only temporary.

Chapter 11

(Changing Reservations)
Business, Money & YOU!

DO NOT SKIP THIS CHAPTER. It may take your life in a totally different direction. Please hear me out. When we are children, we truly dream about what we want to be when we grow up. We had imaginations that were unstoppable. What happens along the way to shrink our dreams and ambitions to a speck of dust? Why does that happen? It happens because we go through school getting bullied or talked down to. We follow a system with cookie-cutter rules that does not allow us to be unique. Some of us live in environments where we may not have supportive parents or family members. You may be told NO for everything you say or do. "Don't touch, it will break." "Don't talk to strangers, it's not safe." "We can't afford that." We are constantly fed fearful information. Our brains don't know how to process the clutter.

I mentioned previously that I had a school guidance counselor who told me to stop by her office to discuss college. I told her I didn't want to go to college. That I didn't think it would be for me. I'll never forget that

Chapter 11

moment when she said, "You'll NEVER amount to anything." I carried that with me for years. I made many of my decisions based on what she said. I am a fighter and a survivor. I won't go down without giving it my ALL. I want this to be a reminder that what you say can and WILL change the course of someone's future, FOREVER. Words are powerful. Honestly, she was probably trying to help me, but it's sometimes not what you say, but how you say it.

After school breaks down, families aren't supportive; so you go to college or get a job. I did go to college. I wanted to use the scholarship money I had earned from earlier pageants. I wanted to learn what I wanted to, not what I had to. Although I'm very non-traditional, sometimes you have to give things a go. I went ahead and fell into the mold of what you are SUPPOSED to do. I learned a lot about life in a short period of time while being in college. When you register for school, you have to include your parent's income whether they are going to help you or NOT.

My dad worked for a cardboard factory and my mom was a manager at fast-food joint. Needless to say, it wasn't a lot. I was denied grants because they made too much money. WHAT? I'm living on my own in Richmond, paying my own rent, feeding myself, and going to school. I met several people driving these nice, expensive cars, but living in subsidized housing for $35 a month and getting their college education paid for. The government has your back; don't worry about anything. Where is the justice in that? I was frustrated and angry. I was tired and hurt. I wanted to scream.

Here's what it taught me. You need to find as many loopholes in the system as you can, have babies out of wedlock, don't get a job, and let the government pay for everything. These were ABLE bodies. I was working three jobs trying to stay in school. I was overtired and mad at the government because people that needed help to better themselves get skipped over because of the silly RULES. I'm the first person to say you should help someone when needed, but when there is a system in place without accountability or responsibility, we have a BIG problem. Something has to change. You need a license to fish, hunt, and drive. Why do you not need a license to have and raise children? The madness needs to stop!

You start a job to pay your bills. You are told when to show up and what you'll be doing, and you have a boss to check your performance. It is sad, but you have probably heard the saying "Your job pays you just enough so you

Chapter 11

don't quit, and you DO just enough not to get fired." Don't get me wrong here. Many of us go out of our way to give the extra smile or make an impression on our clients. I do it because it is WHO I AM. However, people get tired, frustrated, and complacent sometimes. You get in trouble for being ten minutes late, getting sick, not meeting your quotas, or whatever the case may be. We are reminded that they obviously don't see the great things we do for them, so WHY try harder?

The 7 to 10 dollars an hour hardly seem worth it, but you have to live. Now you are beaten down because what you make is NEVER going to be enough to do the things you want to do. Long gone are the days to climb the corporate ladder. There are not enough ladders and who would want to be tied down with so much responsibility that you can't breathe. College kids are coming out of school in droves with less than a bright future with corporate America. Student loans are at an all-time high and our children are drowning because we haven't taught them alternatives. It is our job!

Throughout my life, I watched my mom start numerous businesses on the side, such as Tiara Glass, Princess House, Home Interiors, and many others. She really could sell ice

Life in the Jetstream

to Eskimos. It was impressive. However, it always seemed like more of the money was being put in the "Director's" pocket than hers. I couldn't quite understand that. At age 13, I began to ask questions. How do I get a mortgage? What is insurance for? Show me how to write checks. I guess I was looking for security to later depend on myself. It is NOT normal for kids to ask these questions. However, I am an advocate for children having an understanding of finances and economics in their teens. Download a free copy of questions to ask your teen what they know about finances. My website at www.resultdrivenlife.com

I am grateful to my mother who "TRIED" so many little businesses as an alternate means of income. It taught me a strong work ethic. It also showed me other ways to generate income without having a BOSS. I like to call this thinking outside the box. I did emphasize the word "tried," because what happens is most home-based businesses become a hobby. People spend MORE than they make. The word "try" is such a weak word. Your mind has set you up for failure. The mind believes exactly what you say. What happens next is many people won't believe there is money in the home-based business market because most have only tried and QUIT.

Chapter 11

My whole life I have learned through books how to better myself. There are many of us who want answers. People who want to know why we think like we do. Most of us don't have the thousands of dollars to get educated and get counseling. A book can provide that value if you truly want to help yourself. There are great business books out there. I encourage you to start with Rich Dad Poor Dad by Robert Kiyosaki and read the series, especially The Business of the 21st Century. We need a paradigm shift and it starts with us.

You may be asking why I'm allowing an entire chapter to be about business and money. Almost every day of my life, I hear how everyone needs more money, more time to do what they want, more freedom, and more flexibility. I hear what they are saying. I am grateful that I have been introduced to vehicles that allow me to be a self-promoter in my own time and at my own pace. If I am not where I need to be, it is because of ME. So it is my job to share with as many people as possible. There is another incredible book you need to pick up. This guy has been extremely successful. He is a multi-millionaire with a story to tell. He is humble, modest, a visionary, and a true leader. He inspires me on a weekly basis. I met him several years ago and he became a good friend of mine, Jordan Adler.

Life in the Jetstream

The book is called Beach Money. His book can show you HOW to get the "beach money" you've always wanted.

I hear a lot of people talking, wanting, and asking, but what I don't see is the majority taking ACTION. You can make excuses or you can make money, you can't do both. If you have the income and no quality of life, it's YOUR responsibility to change your situation. If you like having your down time for sleeping in, watching TV, or just hanging out on a weekly basis, then you probably don't really want a change. Have you heard the saying, "Insanity is doing the same thing over and over again, but expecting a different result." We all do this at some point in our lives. Is it your time to WAKE UP?

Your life is a reflection of what you want. If you don't like it, only you can change it. Your mind brings about exactly what you think about. There's another book I recommend. It explains the details of how thinking about what you want works. The book is called "Promptings" by Kody Bateman. Have you ever thought about someone and said you needed to call them, but you never did? Have you heard a song and remembered an old friend and wondered how they were doing? Have you wanted to say good-bye to someone, thinking you would have another opportunity?

Chapter 11

These are called promptings. An inner prompting tells you who you are; the outer prompting tells you what to do with who you are. I have such admiration and respect for Kody. He's a man that truly walks the walk.

Much of our life contains negativity. All the media outlets are talking about death, terrorism, job loss, stock market crash, and downturn in education continually breeds FEAR in society. We are allowing the added turmoil to our daily routines. We should be feeding positivity and enlightenment into our lives because nobody will do it for us. Ask yourself on a daily basis, how you can contribute value to someone else's life every day? We need to be thankful for what we DO have, not focusing on what we don't. We are blessed beyond our wildest imaginations. If you have electricity, indoor plumbing, food on the table, clothes on your back, and a few dollars to spend, then you are WAY ahead of the rest of the world. In Ghana, most don't have indoor plumbing, and around 57 % have no electricity. The infrastructure is less than desirable. It is 2011.Would you think about that in the U.S.?

Our society has set us up to FAIL. Don't let failure be an option. It's part of life if we learn from it. The materialism of needing to have so much money, needing a home with large square footage, needing multiple cars, needing our children to be in private school, buying the latest technology, buying more clothes to store in a closet too full anyway and needing to get our hair and nails done every two weeks. I think you understand where I'm going with this. It will lead you to poverty and loneliness. I know; I was there. It can happen before you realize its coming. Take off your mask and live.

Please humor me just a bit. I'm sure many of you have started getting a product or services to supplement your income at some time in life. Some of us have jumped in full-force, living, eating and breathing an opportunity without taking the steps required to be successful. Many of us have QUIT something in our lives. We don't like rejection. You have five or six people say, "No I'm not interested in what you have," and you gave up. We have a few people complain a product didn't work or it didn't taste right and we say, "Yeah, you're right, I don't think I like it anymore either." We dread telling our family or friends because we know they will think we're foolish.

The crazy thing is we are willing to work 30 years when a pension is NOT in sight. Social security will be a thing of the past. Although we put into it for years, the

Chapter 11

Baby Boomers will suck it dry for the generations to come. No pun intended, it is the way it is. The government never had a plan to secure the income being dispersed over the years. We will work 8 to 14 hours a day to get paid mediocre wages without ANY guarantees of a JOB in the future. Our medical and insurance benefits are harder to get or are even being taken away.

I've learned so many lessons from industry trainers, especially Dani Johnson. She was on the premiere episode of Secret Millionaire. I won't even say if, but WHEN, you get the opportunity go see her LIVE, don't miss out. You don't need to walk there; you need to be in an all-out sprint. Seriously, you should drop everything today and go to the very next First Steps to Success and Creating a Dynasty. Your life will be forever changed. I promise. I don't make many promises. The only one who won't get a thing out of Dani's seminar is someone without a pulse. She is a phenomenal leader and helps us put OUR lives in prospective and balance. Whether you want to or not, your life will change for the better.

Dani has an amazing ability to relate to each of us on a personal level. She has taught me many things, but there are few I want to share with you. She says to the group,

"Weigh your ego against your bank account and see which one weighs more." This means if your pride (ego) stands in the way of being real and transparent, then you need to check "your ego at the door." It is pretty profound when you think about it. Some of us have worried about being in a non-traditional business like Network Marketing, Direct Sales or any home-based business. Why? Are we afraid of what our friends will think? Are we truly going to make any money? Is it appropriate to talk to people of a higher status? Our ego and pride keep us BROKE. We act as if we are insignificant.

You have some doctors or big business owners who would say, "Why should I do something like that? Why should I look at a home- based business when I'm financially successful?" In this day and time, we are not hearing that so much anymore. We have enough successful people who have and are currently validating entrepreneurs. Today, we are in the worst economy and this industry is thriving in a down market.

We have to remember that, doctors are getting hit with huge premiums, mal-practice insurance, and they are tired of being away from their families. They do not enjoy the quality of life they truly desire. They only get paid if they

Chapter 11

show up to work. Our big businesses are struggling with lay-offs, higher costs, and covering employee insurance plans that are through the roof. Many of them are looking to lessen the burden. Mainly, people want to know, "Which company are you working with and how can it benefit my life?" I'm not talking about the CEO's making millions of dollars a year or those with their golden parachutes. You need to watch the documentary with Robert Reich about what happened with our economy over the years and how it evolved. It's an eye- opener.

Let me explain. With traditional small businesses, you spend $50,000 to over 1.5 million dollars for a franchise. In many cases, it takes THREE to TEN years to recoup your initial investment. You work all the time to get it off the ground, you hire employees, and you get paid ONCE for the product or service you offer. Repeat that over and over again, and you have the rat race. Not one person I know would pay that kind of money and only show up for two weeks to six months when starting a business. If NOBODY showed up, they would do WHATEVER it takes to pull business in. They would definitely give it their best shot. Franchises are small businesses and can be very profitable. I know many successful people who have taken this route. Most people don't have that type of income for initial

227

investments.

There are those of us who have come to love an industry that continues to pay you month after month whether you show up or not. It is residual, passive income. This is true leverage at its finest. Why call it anything else? It's a viable business where hundreds of thousands of people realize their dreams. More millionaires have been created through this type of business than any other. Although, it's a double-edged sword. You can purchase YOUR business, normally less than $1000 and most of the time under $500. You earn a commission on every system, product, or service sold. Not ONCE, but over and over again for the one-time sale. The problem with this scenario is that you ONLY paid $500. It's easy to discount as a hobby. You help a few people, they get excited. The business has paid for itself. Now ten to twenty people said NO to you and we justify having spent that money we would have wasted elsewhere.

It is certainly NOT a get-rich-quick process, and if anyone tells you that it is, RUN the other way. It's called creating financial freedom as you go. My job lost its pension plan, so I had to find vehicles that worked for me. Let me say, I too "TRIED" other MLM companies. I failed horribly as well. Why did I fail? I say there are various reasons and a long list of excuses. I want to cover them with you in case you have been in my shoes or are currently looking for another avenue to create income.

The way it was explained to me when I started made it seem like a no-brainer. You invite your friends and family and the dough starts flowing in. WRONG! You may find some resistance with your closet friends and family. Education in the industry is why we fail. Can I show up the first day as an attorney and KNOW exactly what I'm supposed to do? Absolutely not! You need training just like any other job or business. I immediately started off on the wrong track. Most of us become ignorance on fire and start puking all over everyone about how great our company is. Every time they see you coming now they turn around and run because they know ALL you will be talking about is your product or service.

They are amateurs who don't know they are giving the industry a bad name. You have them in every workplace and business. I have been there and I apologize to anyone I've ever offended. The trick to this business is NOT to tell them what you like about it, but to find out their wants and needs. Then find out how to help them reach their goals.

It's about building quality relationships and genuinely caring about how you can better their life. This was a concept that took me many "YEARS" to figure out. With some education you'll be way ahead of the game. Most of us get into a business because we need more money. The way you'll become successful is when you help enough people get what they want.

The overall goal in business is to show people the plan. Either you like it or you don't. Timing may not be right for your life right now and that's OK. I have been in a few NM companies and a few traditional businesses. I have learned so much from each experience. We've also owned two 24 hour gyms and a boutique. I still currently invest into real estate. I finally realized in home-based business, it's only a numbers game. Keep it simple, use the systems and don't reinvent the wheel. We have many successful entrepreneurs who were NEVER sales people or NEVER thought THEY would own a business. Everybody WINS this way!

Having lived on my own since 17, I was very proud of my impeccable credit score. What I didn't realize was how it would change my life down the road. God only knows how much emphasis I have put on having a high score. Life happens and you slowly lose control of your financial situation. We have learned this more now than ever before. Economic times have stretched us ALL to the limit, but many years ago, it brought me to financial ruin. My marriage was on shaky ground, the airline I worked for went bankrupt, which took about 45% of my pay, the taxes in Palm Beach started skyrocketing, the market crashed losing much of my 401K, I lost my pension, and I was back at square one.

My dreams went up in smoke and I had to file for bankruptcy. It was the worst possible thing I could imagine happening at the time, other than dying. Our health and our loved ones being together should be far more important than ANYTHING else. I had worked so hard to be GREAT at as many things as possible and to FAIL miserably with this LABEL. After bankruptcy, people look at you differently, talk to you differently, and you assume that LABEL. I tried immediately after this to start building my credit again. They took one look at my credit report and all of the pages of perfect scores meant nothing in the end. I might as well have tattooed "LOSER" on my forehead. I lived with the guilt and shame of not being prepared enough for the disaster that happened. I'm human. People try to justify that many successful people have been through it, but I didn't care about their situation. It is a

Life in the Jetstream

disgraceful act that didn't have to happen, if I didn't get comfortable.

If you have been through it, believe me, I know hundreds personally that have, there is HOPE! If you are contemplating bankruptcy now, I urge you STOP! Look at ALL other options possible. Get Dani Johnson's War on Debt Program; you can find it at www.warondebtinternational.com. Your life will not be over, but the road is very rough. Dani also makes a great point, that we shouldn't need credit. If we were saving and buying everything with cash we earned as the system intended, we wouldn't end up in that situation.

If you are in financial ruin right now, don't give up. There is life after starting over. It is a long road and a struggle to say the least, but your dreams should NEVER die. It is not the situation that happens to you, it is how we react to that situation. I thank God for making me hit rock bottom to learn a hard lesson. I had others willing to bail me out, but what would I have learned? I needed that to happen in order for me to wake up and see what my life should really be about. It is not about keeping up with the Joneses, or the Kardashians for that matter. Having the huge house with a pool, the cars, the trips, the toys, and

Chapter 11

ALL the extras does not bring happiness. It puts us in a vulnerable spot to lose control. Let me take one step back. If you do not have bills, and you have taken steps to provide for the future, absolutely take advantage of given opportunities.

I've learned to live below our means. Most importantly, my lessons and hardships allowed all of my dreams to come into fruition. It still shocks me. We moved to Virginia, my hometown, so my children would grow up around family. My husband left his job as a police officer and detective to be a stay-at-home dad. That had always been on MY dream list. My kids had been in private school for three years. My 19-year-old is in college and I decided to put my 15-year-old back in public school. I found out public school was offering a two year degree before they finished high school through the AP program. Sometimes you need to do what works best for you.

We took the family home and made it into our sanctuary. I now spend most of my free time in charitable ventures. We actually have a LIFE now. The quality is amazing and if it weren't for all those things happening to me, my life wouldn't be the same today. I sincerely want to see you live a life of peace, abundance, freedom, and prosperity. Embrace what's to come, be diligent, and never lose sight of your DREAMS.

Ask Yourself:

Are you financially stable? Are you prepared if you lose your job tomorrow? Have you tried a home-based business? Are you still searching for a way to generate income? Are you afraid to fail? Have you been financially strapped? What did you learn about money growing up? Can you describe what wealth means to you? Where do you currently spend your money? Do you have enough save for the emergency fund and for rainy days?

Life's Lessons:

My mother taught me to have a strong work ethic. She wanted me to know there was more to life than what her job would offer. I did get the fever early in life. I owned my first business when I was 18 years old. I had a kiosk in the local mall, selling active wear from Hawaii. I knew when I was young I wanted to be a business-owner.

I talk to people today who are counting change until their next paycheck. My job as a coach is not to give you the answers, but to ask enough questions so you get it yourself. Priorities can change when people are ready. How

Chapter 11

many times do you need a door to close on you to realize you should be doing something different? When people tell me they don't have money, and yet answer affirmatively when I ask them if they have a new cell phone, if they get their hair and nails done, if they eat out often, and if they have cable? This already tells me why they don't have money. I have gone into peoples' homes and shown them where to find money. It's everywhere!

Starting a business is a way for you to get ahead. You may have to miss some TV or skip daily social media gatherings to get started. Have you ever heard the saying, "Feast or Famine"? We will go through both a few times in our lives. We just have to prepare for it. I was caught off guard once. I can't tell you how important it is to live below your means, save for the tires that need replacing, and the stove that just burnt out. You'll be glad you did.

Chapter 12

(Glamorous Job in the Sky)
Inside Look into Celebrity Lives

DURING MY FLIGHTS ALL OVER THE WORLD, I HAVE MET some wonderful people and numerous celebrities. Many people loved hearing about my adventures with traveling and which celebrities I've met. This information is about networking, building relationships, how our journey unfolds, and what we can learn from any given situation. I am and continue to be grateful for all the invites I get to events happening all over the world.

I was working a Los Angeles to London flight and met Cher's band. I had talked to her manager, Charlie. He was very gracious to invite me to one of her Las Vegas shows, and I decided to take him up on the offer. Charlie made the arrangements for me, by the time I arrived from London; he was busy with Cher most of the time. He introduced me to Jon Bon Jovi's cousin, Joseph Bon Jovi, who was working on her tour. He asked him to take care of me while he handled Cher for the show. We stayed at the Mirage and the hotel was unbelievable.

Chapter 12

The first night of the show was brilliant. I had front row seats and sat with Sandy Gallin, who was the manager for Sonny and Cher. We went backstage, and Demi Moore was there to meet Cher as well. I met Cher, and Charlie had her autograph a photo for me that said, "Have a safe trip back to London." That photo still hangs in my theatre room today. They made me feel right at home. I went to dinner with the band, played in the casinos, hung out by the pool, and had an amazing time. This story sticks with me for many reasons. A chance meeting on a flight and we had so much in common. Charlie and I stayed friends for years.

I spent Thanksgiving at his home in Hollywood Hills one year. It was Greta Garbo's old home. It was a quaint, unique Spanish-style home with a terrace at the top of the roof, great for entertaining. It takes you back to the 1960's. Charlie is originally from London and had many fond memories. Today, Charlie has founded HUB, otherwise known as Humanity Unites Brilliance. It provides a networking business to fund humanities efforts. He's opened a health and wellness retreat in Sanara Tulum, Mexico and was the first to start a women's empowerment group in Liberia. He continued to pursue his dreams. He also has a new book out called Hear.

Life in the Jetstream

Several years ago, I was fortunate enough to meet Christian Slater and David, his executive assistant and best friend, through a friend of mine in London. Christian was in England performing in, "One Flew Over the Cuckoo's Nest" for six months. Meeting these two was the start of a remarkable friendship. Many people tell you that you have to be in the right place at the right time, and it is so true. I also believe it's not what you know but who you know that will take you in a direction beyond your wildest dreams. This was certainly the case with David and Christian.

I was flying to London on a weekly basis at the time. After having a few conversations with David, I had the opportunity to provide a small favor to him, and he reciprocated with dinner in Piccadilly Circus at a spectacular, unique restaurant. It was during that conversation that we felt comfortable enough around each other to start hanging out on a regular basis. It has always been interesting to me that it has been much easier for me to relate with people from the entertainment field. Our lives mirror each other's with the frequent traveling, staying in many hotels, always being on guard and not knowing whom to trust, among so many other things. The only real difference is they are much better compensated because of their talent or skill. They should be.

Chapter 12

David became a treasured friend. He opened my eyes to a whole other world. I went to Christian's show one night, and there is NOTHING like live theatre. Christian was at the top of his game and was even more brilliant than I imagined. It's not easy performing live, day after day and week after week. I certainly gained a much-deserved respect for his ability to act. More importantly, I found he is a genuine, good-hearted, shy, sensitive guy. His demeanor gave me a new revelation about celebrities. I had met my share throughout my lifetime and after I got to know him, Christian helped me see how human they really are.

I was fortunate enough to spend quite a bit of time with David and Christian in London, as well as in Los Angeles. I was able to visit the guys on the set in Lancaster, California for the movie "Slip Stream." Anthony Hopkins was the mind behind the movie, with several other well-known artists like Jeffery Tambor and Camryn Manheim. This was a wonderful experience for me because the dynamics were very different from those where I had been an extra on several shows. As I mentioned before, being an extra required you to walk on eggshells around everyone: the directors, actors, and so on. As a guest, I felt like a royalty. Christian's star wagon was equipped with a bed, dressing table, and all the cool goodies to make him comfortable. They had vans going to and from the set. Catering was called Craft Services. The actors and crew could have just about anything on demand, such as any style eggs, omelets, meat, fruit, yogurt and a variety of freshly-squeezed juices. The spread was fantastic. David was able to explain some of the lingo in the industry and help me understand the entire process.

The cast was very cordial to me as I sat and watched the filming, although I was probably more of a pain. I asked who, what, and how some of the crew got certain jobs, and also what the job actually was. There is even someone makes sure the script is followed precisely and wardrobe personnel to prep for each scene. I was intrigued by the person whose job is to write every detail down for continuity, complete with photos. There is definitely a creative art in putting a film together. I really enjoyed my time there, understanding more about the work.

I joined them for many dinners or get-together's with the family or for their birthdays at home and at exclusive restaurants. I would never have dreamed of going to the Beverly Hills Hotel, Peppone in Brentwood, or the Bel-Air Restaurant. It was then that I realized we are alike. We all

Chapter 12

have dreams and aspirations, we have jobs to do, we have children to raise, bills to pay, obstacles to overcome, and addictions to be dealt with, among so many other things. The difference for Christian, or ANY other celebrity, is that we don't allow them the privacy to deal with their everyday life. The pressure that is put on them is NOT fair. Yes, they choose to perform and entertain us, but they to want to enjoy some freedoms along the way.

I can recall a time that will be embedded in my mind forever. It is one of the most memorable times in my life to date. My family was planning to come to Los Angeles to meet a mother and her son, K'sun. My husband, Rob was considering a job as his guardian for a TV show in Africa. We were going to spend time with them to see if it was a good fit for both. Before I came to LA, the plan was originally for my family, David, Christian, and his children to go to Magic Mountain. Unfortunately, things change quite often in the entertainment world so that didn't work out. David told me a surprise was in store for us. I'm thinking, "Great! We're getting in for FREE to Magic Mountain! Perfect!

My family was going and we decided to take K'sun Ray, the child actor we were there to visit, as well. It was

241

Life in the Jetstream

interesting because my family lived in Virginia, and K'sun in Malibu. He had NEVER been to Magic Mountain and had ALWAYS wanted to go. I was surprised he hadn't been because he had been on many shows by this time. I thought they certainly could afford to go. We did not MapQuest how to get there. K'sun knew exactly where to go though he had never been. We were amazed. We played a game on the ride over to Magic Mountain called, "Is it bigger than a bread box" until we were close to the park.

We arrived at the park and were told to go to VIP parking. We pulled up in front and were met by a VIP representative. I was then told that Christian wanted us to enjoy a VIP day at Magic Mountain. What? I was blown away. I didn't really know what that meant yet, but to have VIP parking and someone escort us through the gate I was beside myself. It was if we have Christian with us. We were escorted into the park before everyone else and started the tour in the gaming section. We played several games for everyone to win some prizes. I noticed the VIP rep, Andrew, kept writing what looked like checks every time we played a game. I got nervous thinking we were adding to Christian's tab. I asked Andrew to make sure it didn't cost anymore, because I wasn't supposed to know how much this day really cost. It was his gift.

242

Chapter 12

I was thrilled as we entered the park aware of our good fortune. I felt like a little kid in the biggest toy store EVER. Christian will never truly know what a GIFT he bestowed on all of us that day. We had three humongous bags of toys and stuffed animals. I had almost forgotten to call and say thank you right away. The VIP had us on a mission and we were off to the races. I believe I got a call from David, as we were getting on our second roller coaster. It was an unforgettable experience. We rode all the roller coasters, even getting on them over and over again in the front row. We also had a private cabana at Splash Mountain, and they gave us towels and sun-block to take home with us. They also gave us all the food we could eat. I was astonished to have such an eventful day, yet be so relaxed and not rushed with everything we did that day.

After swimming, sliding, and lying out for a few hours, we were ready to hit the park again. The day wasn't over yet because there was another surprise in store for us. They had to get us to the back of the park because the parade was getting ready to start. That's when they told us WE were the GRAND MARSHALLS. Oh my goodness! It was so fast that we didn't have time to digest it. I looked like a complete mess. NO make-up, I had been swimming, was drenched in sweat from the heat, and I'm going to be

Life in the Jetstream

waving to everyone. That's a woman thing. They were probably wondering what this family was doing up there. We certainly didn't have a clue. Then it was time to go home. We made our last stop to get Dippin' Dots for the ride. We all were in awe of what a great time we had and how we would never forget it. It was magical.

The next morning my family had planned on going to see David and Christian for a BBQ. What we didn't expect was to meet with an infamous TV psychologist in the home of where we were staying in Malibu. We were getting to know K'sun, the child actor. His mother had made arrangements to have a group meeting so would get to know each other. David was calling to see when we would arrive and said that we needed to hurry or we wouldn't get the other surprise. WOW! How many surprises can you have in one weekend? I don't know if my heart can handle it. Finally the session ended and we ran out the door. It took some coaxing for K'sun's mom to agree to let him go with us so he could thank Christian personally.

We were driving from Malibu to Beverly Hills, which seemed like it took forever. We finally made it to the house. My children at that point had never met Christian's children, Jaden and Eliana. That was the surprise. They

Chapter 12

never told me the kids would be there to play together. He had them there so they all could swim and play while we barbecued. I had brought a lot of the toys that we won at Magic Mountain to give them to Jaden and Eli. We all went swimming, had a BBQ, watched Eli put on a show for us with the new stuffed animals, hung out, and just had fun. What a great way to wrap up a weekend.

To this day, my children say it's their most memorable experience, along with their four and a half month stay in Africa with K'sun. My husband stayed almost six months in Africa as K'sun's guardian on the TV show, "Life Is Wild." This adventure is another book or maybe a movie in itself. This became a crucial time in my life as we were getting to know the young man we now call our "adopted son." The plot has so many twists and turns, ups and downs, exasperating moments, and chilling tales. A Hollywood story revealed as a Lifetime feature. Who knows; it may eventually come your way if the time is right.

About six months earlier, I had met a girl and her mother who were on vacation in LA. I was working as flight crew and staying in the Sheraton hotel. Many times while in LA, I tried to see different friends. I had rented a car and didn't make a plan before I arrived this time. I ran into Jennifer H. and her mother and started talking to them. I found out it was their first time in LA. They were from South Carolina and had the cutest accents. The rental cars were sold out, so they were stuck. I offered to show them around and gave them my room number, then changed to go out. They gave me a call and we hit the town together.

It was Oscar weekend, and we ran into traffic as I was taking them to see the Hollywood sign. We stopped by my good friend Tom's house. He's a cosmetic dentist in Beverly Hills. We ate at Denny's in the UCLA area. Jen and I laugh so hard now about going to Denny's since LA is so well-known for great, hip places, even outdoor cafés. I had talked to David on the phone and put him on the line with Jen when I was trying to navigate around the chaos. They talked for almost an hour. David even talked to her mother. I was thinking, "What in the world do they have in common?" but David is a master of being able to relate with others. She's in her last year of college, so sweet and naïve, and he's traveled the world with Christian, seeing and doing what most only read about.

I needed to fly back home but was returning to LA two days later. They still couldn't get a rental car so I let them borrow mine for the next two days until I returned. As a

Chapter 12

flight attendant, don't make plans or you'll be disappointed. I flew through Chicago, got stuck in a snow-storm, and didn't make it back to LA. Jen and Sherry took the car back for me when they were going back home to South Carolina. I was so worried when they were driving around LA because they were new to the area, but I was more afraid if something happened with the car because I didn't initially tell my husband about it. I did have a good reason though. Rob was on location in Johannesburg, South Africa, and we didn't talk often. I felt I couldn't explain everything via e-mail before the car was back anyway. Thank God it all worked out.

There is one last thing I want to share with you about my experience with David and Christian. Making memories is far more important than having material things. The guys invited me to New York to go to the LIVE EARTH concert. It was being simulcast in nine countries all over the world. This was a monumental event with hundreds of talented musicians playing in this concert. I flew to New York and hopped a cab to Christian's place. The guys had to go out for a meeting so I took a short nap until they came back. They said a few others were going to join us as well. Another surprise for me as Jen H. and her friends showed up.

The reason I'm telling you this story is you never know who you'll meet, why your paths crossed, what will happen, how friendships are created, and how lives go in a totally different directions. When you read on, you can see how many things tie in. While I was in New York at Christian's place about six months after we met, Jen H. was coming to meet up with David for the first time. It was wild to have her share this experience with us.

The guys had arranged a limousine to pick us up to go to the concert. I was happy to see Jen. I was even happier thinking there might be a love connection between her and David. We headed to the VIP tents where there were big screen TV's, a huge bar, comfy sofas all around, and air conditioning. Jen and I were able to catch up. We were all able to hang out and have a little fun. Christian had a few interviews to do before joining us again. We all had a good time and never seemed to be able to make it to our designated seats for the concert.

I had a blast, and from that point on, David and Jen stayed together for almost 5 years. I met Jen in LA for lunch about 3 and half years into the relationship. I had seen and talked to her during that time briefly, but it was only now that I made the connection. I met her when she was finishing college. She was very young and beautiful. She is still beautiful today, but in such a short time, she evolved into a strong, spirited, independent, and spiritual woman. Her goals are similar to mine: to help make the world a better place one person at a time. We can somewhat relate with our backgrounds as well. Since she has been dating David, she has traveled the world with both David and Christian. She has seen and done what most only dream about. Jen knows one of my favorite sayings is "LIVING the DREAM" and that's what we do. She truly understands my meaning now. You never know what is possible with the people you meet.

David and Christian, I thank you so much for sharing your life and allowing me to experience many firsts. I thought I had experienced so much already. I learned a lot about myself along the way. Christian, I have a new respect for "celebrities," child actors, and you as a human being. You are kind and gracious with so much to offer the world, as well as being extremely talented. I appreciate your willingness to offer yourself for charitable ventures and helping me in so many ways. You are truly one of a kind. I'm so proud of your accomplishments. I hope the world will see the same in you.

Life in the Jetstream

David, you became such a close friend. It was a whirlwind adventure. You let me into your life, gave me an understanding of the entertainment industry and your private world. It was several years of good times, serious conversations, trying different foods, enjoying finer restaurants, and walks in the park. You'll always have a special place in my heart. I pray we all find our way home.

I know many people love celebrity stories. That's because most people put celebrities on a pedestal. They think they live a life of fame, money, power, and prestige. They do, to a certain extent, but they pay the ultimate price. They have no privacy or freedoms. They struggle to find people who like them for who they are and not what they portray on TV. They get ridiculed for any accidental mishaps because they are in the public eye. In the end, they are JUST like us. We can appreciate their talent and skill on screen. They are humans taking their own personal journey through this thing called LIFE!

Ask Yourself:

What does being a celebrity mean to you? If you could meet any celebrity, who would it be and why? Have you had a celebrity encounter? Was it a terrific experience?

Chapter 12

Life's Lessons:

Television and movie actors, athletes, singers, and other entertainers still have dreams. Actors struggle with not knowing whether a show will be cancelled. If an athlete gets hurt, his career may be over. They live with uncertainty every day, just like you and me. Believe it or not, many of them have low self-esteem. They have faced more rejection than we could imagine. Choose not to idolize what you see on TV. Realize there is a celebrity in all of us. You have the power to make your life anything you choose.

Chapter 13

(Amazing GIFT of Flight)
A Heart to Give

WE SPEND OUR LIVES WONDERING HOW WE CAN MAKE A DIFFERENCE. We want to be a part of something bigger than ourselves. One of my favorite songs truly says what I feel in my heart. It's, "Legacy" by Nichole Nordeman.

The lyrics go something like this: "I don't mind if you have something nice to say about me. And I enjoy an accolade like the rest. I want to leave a legacy. How will they remember me? Did I choose to love? I want to make a mark on things; I want to leave an offering of mercy and grace unapologetically." I know I have been truly blessed in my life beyond my wildest dreams and it's getting even better. It's time to give back.

We don't have to wait until we have ALL that we want or need in order to start giving. For years I used to say to myself, if only I could get to this point, I can give more or do more. I can focus more energy on what my heart says to do. I heard this voice one day and he said, "WHY WAIT?" Start today! There is not going to be a better time than now.

Chapter 13

We are not promised tomorrow.

I was living in Palm Beach, Florida. I wanted my children to understand the meaning of giving and why it's important. I'm grateful to have children compassionate enough to want to help others in need. I don't know if the need to give comes from within or is a learned behavior. I know it ran deep in me before I knew what it meant. I started taking my son, Austin, to the Children's Home Society, delivering stuffed animals and talking to some of the kids and facilitators. I wanted to know the reasons some of the children were there: they were abandoned, the mother had AIDS, some parents died, the parent was in prison, guardian in rehab, and some of the children were just in transition.

One incident changed my son forever. We headed to a nursing home on Mother's Day with almost 200 roses to pass out. I look at the elderly as "The Forgotten Ones." They rarely get visitors, have lived a life, and have such wisdom we don't understand. As Americans, it's been our culture to let them fade away in the nursing homes, as if they didn't exist.. Those that have a heart for the elderly please step up and become a visitor, a reader for them, a volunteer for game times, or whatever you can do with

Life in the Jetstream

what time you have. An hour a week to someone without a single visitor speaks volumes.

Austin and I started out delivering the roses to each woman throughout the nursing home, whether she was a mother or not. They have all influenced another woman in their life before. I decided I would show him what to do and then allow him to continue until finished. He was very quiet and shy. I would offer the rose, say Happy Mother's Day, and ask how she was. Sometimes I would give hugs or talk awhile longer if they choose to keep engaging with me. They loved seeing a child come through the door and acted as if they hadn't seen one in years. They wanted to give him hugs as well, and although reluctant, he allowed a few to hug him.

We had finished giving roses to all the main nursing home patients. Then we proceeded to the psychiatric side of the nursing home. We initially did the exact same thing. One woman even put the rose stem sideways in her mouth as if she were a dancer doing the tango. As we were completing our rounds, this woman came shuffling her feet as fast as she could across the floor to get to us. My son ran behind my leg to hide. She handed me a toothpick. I thanked her and gave her a hug. It was remarkable! They

Chapter 13

think she was not in her right mind, but to give me something back after we had given her a gift showed me she had them fooled. I had to explain to my son that she was only trying to offer us a kind gesture in return for giving her something. Nevertheless, he no longer wanted to visit nursing homes.

We also were fortunate to have Patricia and Jefferson, a mother and son from Quito, Ecuador, stay with us for six weeks. They were in the U.S. getting treatment at the Shriner's Hospital. Jefferson had a disease called Fanconi syndrome. It's a vitamin D deficiency in the blood cells that make the bones weak, which has caused him to have rickets. An acquaintance of mine knew my heart for charity and knew to let me know if there was a need. She couldn't personally house them so she called me.

Although Jefferson was older than my son, he was much smaller. We had a language barrier, as Patricia didn't speak any English. My Spanish was broken, but we made it through. Our kids had a great time together, but eventually I had to put them on a flight back to Quito. My husband was a trooper because he didn't share the same feelings, at the time, about my need to save the world. It took him years of conditioning and knowing me to understand the importance.

I had also started a non-profit 501(c)3 charitable organization. It was called Celebrity Choice Foundation. I had some wonderful people help get it established, do the articles and sit on the board. I found huge lessons that would discourage me over the next few years. All I wanted to do was get in the trenches, get my hands dirty, and work one-on-one with those in need. I wanted to give hope to the hopeless, food to the hungry, clothes to the disaster victims, and encourage kids at risk. I chose to work with numerous celebrities because most people felt they were lost causes. They also have influence to reach others and make a bigger impact.

I was truly honored to work with St. Jude Children's Research Hospital, I Have A Dream Foundation, Adam Walsh's Children's Fund, Children's Home Society, Big Brothers Big Sisters, and actually too many others to name them all. What I found are a lot of people working together to make people's lives better. What I also found is most people have no idea where to start. The unfortunate part of my venture is that volunteer's only wanted to participate with the celebrities. I found myself doing all of the groundwork, the organizing, paperwork, phone calls, and

Chapter 13

other grunt work.

I did manage to get help when going to children's hospitals delivering stuffed animals, as well as assistance in helping gather clothes and toiletries for natural disasters. I realized Charity is not really charity. The government sees it as a BUSINESS. The information, paperwork, and record keeping finally set me off, as I had put in so much of my time and money. Fundraising becomes hard when you are not well established. I said there has to be a better way. I am grateful to all the celebrities that participated. It was an amazing experience for all the kids that participated.

I have to mention that the one I was most impressed with was Wynonna Judd. I had five kids from the "I Have A Dream Foundation" participate. These were at-risk kids with parent problems, truancy issues, and bad influences. Their director, Chris, was amazing because she would have conversations about Wynonna before they arrived. Wynonna opened up her tour bus, allowed everyone to sit and talk about their aspirations. This was such a treat for these kids. I remember one of the children asked her why she rode a Harley. She said, "It's not because I'm a rebel, it's because it makes me feel free." She also gave them a book to take away. Time is the most valuable thing you can

Life in the Jetstream

give a child. Wynonna was asking them questions, which made them feel as if she TRULY cared.

When my husband had the opportunity to live in South Africa for 6 months, my children had joined him for four months. We were able to see the extreme need for shoes. It's something we take for granted every day. Some of us have 20 to 30 pair. How could it be that some of the children were lucky enough to go to school with mandatory uniforms, but many didn't have any shoes? I had approached production about what we could do to get shoes brought here and send them to the villages. A few of us checked into it and found that we were not allowed in the villages unless we had shoes for everyone, as it would start a riot. This was discouraging because it was only revealed as we were leaving Africa that we found out certain organizations acquire shoes and hold them until they have enough for each person.

Later, the airline I'm with brought us back to Africa. However, I found Ghana very different than South Africa. The infrastructure was less than desirable. You saw much more poverty there and learned that the people would do just about anything to make some money. This was my first time witnessing all the men and women on the streets with huge plastic packs of wares they were selling from the tops of their heads. They would sell water packs, chips, toilet paper, and maps to tourists as you leave the airport. You name it they were beating feet trying to sell it. On the beach, they would sell art work and jewelry, they would try to give you a manicure or a pedicure, or they would even braid your hair. I've seen a lot of stuff all over the world, but here everyone was working just to eat.

I did start spending time at an orphanage in Ghana. It broke my heart to see the living conditions. Yet they were so happy when you would sit with them, sing with them, or play ball with them. They were really excited when I brought them a picture of the group because they could see themselves for the first time. We take for granted the millions of photos we have available to us. It's astounding. It's the simple things that matter. They were interested in seeing photos of my family, too. I'd watch them eat porridge every day, trying to figure out a way for them to have chickens or to raise them so they would have other options. They were cooking outside on a little pot.

I started bringing two of the girls with me on the layovers to the hotel. I would get their hair done, buy swim suits to swim in the pool, or take them to dinner, although they had a hard time eating anything else. The porridge was such a staple in their diet that it was hard for them to adjust. They would pack the extra food into napkins to take back to the orphanage so all could share with them. We would walk the beach and talk about what dreams were to them. What they wanted and how things could be different. I enjoyed these conversations because I learned what they desired. I remembered them telling me the elders decided whom they would marry. They said they wanted to marry someone rich. I said what do you mean by that? Who is rich? They said, "If you have a JOB, you're rich." WOW! If you had a car, you were very rich.

They loved taking baths, watching local TV, and enjoying the little snacks I brought them throughout the day. It was the little things they didn't get to enjoy on a daily basis. I remember when I would go to the orphanage to visit, I would let them know I coming. Gloria would wait for me outside and run in front of my driver so excited I was there. Gloria's best friend, Shelia was later adopted and lives in Florida. I still keep in touch with her as well.

For Christmas of 2011, my husband and I flew to Ghana for seven days to have Christmas with the kids. I had six suitcases of things I was taking to the children.

Chapter 13

Shoes for everyone and gifts they could use to play with others. My original plan was to have all the kids from the orphanage come to my hotel. There were 35 kids and three adults. I'd have the buses pick them up as I had everything pre-approved at the hotel prior to my arrival. All of the children, with the exception of the girls that came to visit, had never seen a hotel.

Unfortunately, about a week before we arrived, a 12-year-old girl drowned in the pool. The staff was still going to allow us the courtesy, even though they were very reluctant. Rob and I decided we would take everything to them. I was having a cake made that said, "Happy Birthday Jesus!" I was worried that once my husband saw where we would be driving to, he wouldn't allow me to go back. It was not safe. There are no road signs or ways of figuring out how to get back if something happened. That's the police officer in him. He wouldn't want me going by myself, but most of the crew doesn't want to visit orphanages on their down-time.

We made it to the home and were happy to see everyone. Rob met as many children as he could. They wanted to show me around the new place. Afterwards, we decided to sing "Happy Birthday" to Jesus and cut the cake.

It was a highlight for all of us. After passing out the shoes and gifts, I sat and talked with the girls and Rob got up and started playing ball with the boys. They loved getting that little bit of attention.

To me, Christmas is not about the material gifts you get or give in the season. We have been sold that lie. We get into debt giving things that people don't even like and feel the need to impress those that don't really care. Why? I have celebrated it as Jesus's birth and give to those who can't give back. That's GIVING! My children have never seen lots of gifts under our tree. Many years, we've been in other countries for the holidays. I was raised less fortunate. Thankfully it helped me not go overboard. I wanted my kids to know they only get two gifts. I allowed them to believe in Santa. One was from him and one was from us. To this day, they get only two gifts. I'm not saying you need to be like me, but think about how you won't be stressed out after the holidays. Tell your friends or family who you usually buy gifts for that you are choosing to give to someone who doesn't have as much as they do, and hope they understand. You can change your traditions starting this year, if you want to.

On many occasions, I picked families in need to give to,

Chapter 13

if it's on my heart. When something is on my heart there is a tugging to act or help in a situation where those families might not experience any act of kindness. This year was no different. Sometimes you hear of or are reminded of people to see or call. That's a prompting that you need to get in touch with them. When you have the need to give, something tells you that you need to do this. I was leaving for Dubai with my family for Christmas of 2013. I was driving home from the store and had an overwhelming feeling to stop by a house that was on my way home.

It was dark, raining, the house was dilapidated, and I didn't know how anyone was living there. I started to panic, thinking: why do I have to stop, what am I going to say, should I say I'm from the church, should I call my pastors wife and see what to do? I start hitting my steering wheel, saying, "Really, do I have to do it today?" I knew the answer to that, so I stopped. I don't remember much of what was said other than introducing myself as a neighbor. I asked about the kids as I could see three of them playing in the kitchen floor. I had been meaning to stop by this house for about four months after seeing two of the children get off the bus. I never stopped, until now.

I had been crying after I left the home and walked into

my house. Rob could immediately notice something was wrong. I told him what happened and he said, "Let's go shopping now." It was 9:30 p.m.at night. We are leaving the next day for Dubai. I had already told the family I would not be back till after Christmas, that I'd see them then, and she said it was okay. I knew when Rob said, "Let's go," that it needed to be then.

We picked up everything the mom had put on the wish list. I went home and started wrapping the gifts. On each name-tag, I wrote their name and "from JESUS!" I had a friend who said he could deliver them on Christmas Eve. He left all the gifts in a large trash bag outside their door. Some of the best gifts in the world are the ones you give anonymously, just from the heart.

I have a vision of making the world a better place. Many of us grow up wanting to make a difference in the lives of others. Why is that? I believe that for me, having been in so many bad situations in the past, I felt blessed as an adult and it was my turn to pass it on. I have always loved the movie, "Pay it Forward." It is a must-see movie. It's about doing good deeds for others and having them do something nice for someone else. It was a movement a child started that didn't get to see it to fruition. We could

Chapter 13

change the world if we all would do a very small part. It is sometimes difficult to think that ONE person can make a difference, but I promise you, YOU CAN! Some of my influencers are Mother Teresa, Martin Luther King, Jr., the Dalai Lama, Gandhi, and Oprah. What would the world look like today without their contributions?

You watch infomercials of the children starving in all these third world countries but never realize many are hungry in our own backyard. We see earthquakes, tsunamis, hurricanes, and tornados completely devastate in America. The diseases killing us today are one's we can prevent for the most part. Heart disease, cancer and diabetes are the main cause of MOST deaths. Let's be a country that works by being pro-active. Childhood obesity is at an all-time high. When I heard that our generation will be the first to outlive our children, I was speechless. We are inundated with a wealth of FREE information on the internet about better food options, activities to keep us in shape, and overall better health advice.

The reason I'm telling you this story is not for a pat on the back. I know we all have empathy and compassion and want to share that. I want you to be able look at your own situation and discern whether you should take that step of faith. I'm sure there have been many times when we said, "Yeah, I'd like to serve at a soup kitchen, I'd like to help the elderly, I'd like to give some of my things to those that need it more." Whatever you feel you like to or want to do. JUST DO IT! There is something in each of us that wants to make the world a better place but you don't know where to start, I have a list of things that are FREE, while some require time or money. See what works for you. Visit my webpage at www.resultdrivenlife.com.

I know there are so many valuable and highly effective charities around. I am only going to share some of them with you. Several have become near and dear to me. I want you to start somewhere, so you'll find the list in the 10 Ways to Thrive in Turbulent Times, in the Giving Back section.

Ask Yourself:

Have you ever been in need? What does your heart say about giving? Do you currently contribute to or support a cause? What changes can you make today to help someone else? What kind of legacy will you leave?

Life's Lessons:

Charity work is where I felt I could make the most

Chapter 13

difference and change the world. What happened was that it changed me. I was selfish, because it made ME happy and I felt good when I could do for others. Don't get involved in a worthy cause for a pat on the back. You'll be disappointed. Do it because you enjoy it or because it's fulfilling a deeper purpose.

Chapter 14

(Flying through the Storms)
Healing the Past and Vicious Cycles

WE SPEND OUR LIVES SEARCHING FOR A WAY TO HEAL from our past regrets and mistakes. We torture ourselves day in and day out. We impose our beliefs on everyone that crosses our path. Our goal is to connect with others on a more intimate level to have real relationships. The purpose of relationships is to be healed, and healing can only occur when our wounds are revealed. Then your ego is confronted with a catch-22. If I don't show myself, there can be no growth within. This is where we get "STUCK."

On the other hand, if I honestly reveal myself, I can be judged, found unattractive, and my friends or spouse may not want to stay around me. How many of you want relationships that have some depth? When people judge you, they are not willing to look within themselves to be authentic. This is definitely a time when you personally want to move through your healing process and not worry about others. People need us to relate to them, not judge them. What kind of example are we?

Chapter 14

We are not bad people. We are wounded and in need of our own transformation. The important thing about our past is not what happened, but what we have done with what happened. What did we learn from the situation, how did we grow from it? I did not question God about why something happened. I did ALWAYS ask what do you want me to learn from it? In most cases, it was revealed. One of the main reasons I decided to write this book was because God put in my heart years ago that it's a way for others to HEAL through my story. What's interesting is when you write a book like this, it can truly help you heal and feel free to talk about your experiences openly. It's not easy laying all your cards on the table. My hope is that if my story can change someone else's script to make it better, my job is complete. We can find hope and healing through others if we allow ourselves to.

I personally had let my thoughts become the demons that I faced daily. My addictions became the emotional baggage I have carried around for years. I acted out all of my setbacks and misfortunes by playing the victim. I take full responsibility for my role in how I have acted. If I have mistreated someone or if I spoke rudely to or about you, I ask for your forgiveness. Each of us needs to move away from that space and decide that we're choosing freedom over bondage. I want and surely embrace CHANGE. People don't necessarily fear change, people fear what change will or won't bring. The expectation of loss is when the change is done.

Emotional baggage will block physical, spiritual and financial success. It affects all aspects of your life. Regardless of what you learn, believe, and choose in your life, we still need to be held accountable for our actions. Take responsibility. Healing takes time. My life has had various peaks and valleys. The valleys or depth of my tragedies did not allow me a "GET OUT OF JAIL FREE CARD." What does that mean? Don't ask for sympathy for what you've been through. Another great quote is a reminder, "Nobody cares how many storms you've encountered, but did you bring in the ship?" People only want to see how you came through it. My faith is what carried me. When I was crying, God held my hand. When I fell, he picked me up. When I was lost, he showed me the way.

I come across stories that impact me every day. I am aware that what you speak can and will appear. I can best relate to the scriptures. "Life and death is in the power of the tongue, and as a man thinks in his heart, so is he. There

Chapter 14

is POWER in words that can bring life and death. First, let me say I honor whatever your beliefs are or are not. I have friends from all walks of life. These are spiritual truths regardless of beliefs.

When you speak about negative things, more of it shows up in your life. When you focus on the positives, it's always brighter. You've heard the saying "Misery loves company," so remember what you speak about you bring about. I told you previously no matter how much peace and joy you have in life, we will constantly face challenges. We won't be immune to it. We will be better equipped to handle it. The other reality is people will do what you do. You may say one thing, but do another. We need to be the example and let our lights shine everywhere. Guard your thoughts and words carefully. This may include what you watch, what you listen to, and who you hang out with.

My husband was talking to a woman whose basement got flooded and everything was ruined. She said to my husband that she prayed to clean up the mess in her basement, but that wasn't the way she wanted it done. She was completely distraught. A few days later, he returned to the home. The woman saw my husband and began to cry, and he asked, "What's the matter?" She began to explain that her daughter was very sick years ago and she kept asking to take her pain away until one day, the unthinkable happened. The daughter took her own life. The mother had endured such a painful experience for many years. Many of the things in the flooded house were the daughter's belongings that her mother did not want to get rid of. My husband gave her a hug and said, "It's TIME!" Healing starts now. He told her to find a church, a support group, or someone she could talk to. Let go, your daughter would want you to move on.

My heart is anguished from situations and events that happened before I was even born. I want to heal and repair some of the damage done that continues to live on in each generation. I'm so sorry that there was slavery right here in my own backyard. I recently watched the film 12 Years A Slave. I watched several movies about slavery, the abolitionists, and the activists. Many of these people I have come to admire and respect, such as Martin Luther King Jr., Rosa Parks, and Maya Angelou. I did not wear those shoes, and I was not made to feel the way they did. I can't even imagine the pain and agony of that kind of abuse or injustice. I offer my sincere apology on behalf of the ENTIRE human race that took part.

Chapter 14

I experienced some of this behavior in South Africa about seven years ago. The Dutch were still treating the people as if apartheid never happened. It was appalling. One of our favorite movies is The Power of One with Morgan Freeman. It's an older movie, but it's so amazing. It will change your perspective. We had the opportunity to go to Sun City in Africa. We heard about the song Michael Jackson wrote about NOT going to Sun City when he was fighting for the rights of the people. Sun City has a few awesome palaces and a beautiful water park. There are many vacation spots there, but obviously they are for the wealthy. The song was a plea to not go and visit so they could stand for FREEDOM of the people.

I can go into several events that my heart aches for, but I will mention only a couple of them. I lift all Jewish people up and all of our veterans, old and new. I have traveled throughout the world and have seen some heinous things. I've walked where part of history once was and cried for the people and their families who suffered during those times. It's heartbreaking after walking through the Anne Frank home in Amsterdam trying to imagine what that could have been like. Just to watch Schindler's List was more than I could bear.

Also to our veterans, I realize FREEDOM isn't really FREE. Someone paid a price. I have spent time with some of the soldiers from Wounded Warriors. I was taking them back to the battlefield for closure. They were missing eyes, legs, and arms. Some were joking just to hold back the terror they faced from knowing they were confronting their fears. I've heard stories of wives leaving them and friends walking away because they were more of a burden than anything. Forgive us! My prayer is that we reach out and touch each other, support our neighbors and friends. We need compassion and that only comes from LOVE. Love is what we are born with and fear is what we've learned.

It seems so trivial to me sometimes when I think of people saying, "Life's too busy, my job stinks, my husband or wife is a pain, I need more money," or whatever it may be. I do my best to look at the bigger picture and not involve myself with the meaningless things that bring you down for no reason.

I mentioned briefly before that I am a real estate investor. My husband and I had just finished a remodeling project after several months. We decided to put this home on the market with a realtor so I could finish this book. The second day on the market, our home was burglarized. The

Chapter 14

perpetrators kicked the door in and stole all the brand new appliances and air conditioning unit. My husband called to tell me about it. I was in Florida visiting family. I was at my brother-in-law's house talking to him as it was the first time I could see him in months. He had cancer and was going through chemo and radiation. He lost tons of weight and was still taking care of the family financially. His immune system was weak, and we weren't able to visit for quite a while. After I left Doug and Rhonda's home I called my husband to tell him, "Don't worry about the appliances, they are all replaceable." When you spend time with someone who has the possibility to lose their life and is fighting a battle, material things don't mean so much.

Your circumstances do not define you unless you let them. When you are carrying all of this emotional baggage, it will block your spiritual, physical, and financial success. It can and will affect how much we earn, what we believe, and how we choose. It's all up to you! I thank God for all the tests I've been put through. It taught me to get over myself. We stand in our own way.

Deciding to heal, move on, and walk away from the past is a choice, YOUR CHOICE. We can be a part of the solution or a part of the problem. We can choose to love or

275

choose to remain in fear. Fear can be seen as anger, abuse, disease, obsession, addiction, selfishness, corruption, bitterness, and violence. Fear is also a lack of understanding. We are often taught that it's comfortable to walk in the understanding that we are familiar with.

Vicious Cycles:

I want everyone to understand how this chapter might fit in YOUR life. Our lives are a reflection of all that happened before we were even born. It's hard to believe, but our ancestors can give us answers and help guide us in our future. Remember, I am a Christian and have total faith in God. We call these generational curses. It means that we can continue to pay for the sins of our fathers. That's why I believe my ancestors can give us answers. The reason I say that is you can track your family history, and in most cases, it ALWAYS repeats itself. Few of us are willing to track or seek our backgrounds in fear of what we'll find. I have watched it happen over and over again, not just with my family alone. Knowledge is POWER. Ignorance is NOT bliss.

I found it interesting when Ancestry.com came out. There was a documentary about 2 different men and their lives. One was from high society and the other was an

Chapter 14

outlaw from the Wild West. They shared the genealogy and the links from the two. In the case of the high society guy, all the family members had great educations. In the case of the outlaw, not one family member finished school. The high society family had great jobs as lawyers, bankers, and business men. For the outlaw's family, the jobs were as thieves, miners, and philanderers.

Let me give you some examples. I didn't learn to communicate growing up. I didn't know anything about my family. My mother and the three generations of children before her were all given away to other family members to be raised. They also were ALL sexually abused. They ALL had been estranged from most of their family members. They ALL married alcoholics. They ALL died relatively young with the exception of my mother. They ALL lived with a poverty mindset. The list goes on and on. However, my mom stopped a few of the cycles. Although she had no idea that was what she was doing, it helped in other areas of our lives.

It was the words her mother-in-law spoke that stopped the pattern of abandoning us. Her mother-in-law was mean to her throughout the marriage; however my mom went to visit her on her death-bed. My mom was considering giving all of us, her three children, away because she had no way to take care of us. She didn't have a job, and my biological dad was living with another woman. Mom had nowhere to go and no one to turn to. At my grandmother's hospital bed, Pat told my mother she would eat salt and drink water before she'd ever give up her kids. That night, she made a decision to keep her children together no matter what. Her sole purpose in life is to keep the family together. I admire that. The more you know about your family history, the easier it will be to break some of those patterns. We are destined for greatness, so it's time to claim it. Your can change history or repeat it.

Many of you may have made choices you didn't want to make. Quit beating yourself up about what's happened and decide to do something about it if you're not happy. There are so many variables to have a happy, productive life. Choose happiness! There is not one person, one place, or any one thing that can make you happy. We think our friends, spouses, our jobs, or the places we go should be able to make us happy. Guess what? If you're unhappy, you are the common denominator.

I'm a BIG fan of the movie "A Knight's Tale," with Heath Ledger. It's about a young boy who came from the

Chapter 14

poorest part of town, yet his father had such dreams for him. He gave him away so his son could have a better life and learn a skill. He became a knight, but unfortunately he wasn't of nobility. As many circumstances can be unusual in our lives, his was no different. Something magical happened in the midst of the turmoil and he was able to change his stars. There is a message for all of us. Basically it is this: never give up! We can do or be ANYTHING we desire.

My philosophy is: if you don't like the odds, change them. I looked at everything negative in my genealogy and worked on making it a positive. It has been a real challenge. Once I feel like I conquered one area, I get hit hard by the next issue. I know this is God's way of building my character and molding me to make me stronger. I am disappointed in many of my decisions from the past, but my life is better because of it. We're allowed to make mistakes if we learn from them. Sometimes it took me having many bad relationships to recognize the good ones. I made many rotten financial decisions to learn that I can't be trusted with more if I can't handle what I currently have. We will be given gentle nudges to learn lessons, but if we don't recognize the gentle reminders we will be given a more intense opportunity. I look at my failures as such a gift.

It is in our best interest to learn about our past. We all have some dysfunction to a certain extent. For some, it is much more overwhelming than others. There are women I know today who remain introverts because they don't feel they were given enough attention throughout their life. People were hurt in the past and never given a sounding board to get through the pain. Teens want to take their lives not just because of the bullies, but because they feel they have nowhere to turn or no one to depend on. Some wealthy parents are enabling their children, handing them EVERYTHING and not giving them proper survival tools. People today appreciate and need YOUR TIME, so much more than they need material things.

It's important not only in young relationships, but in all relationships, to communicate where you are in life. Marriages are easily broken because we don't know enough about each other. Don't be afraid to ask questions, to ask about family members, and to see how the other feels about having children or not having them. What kind of issues is your partner dealing with and what are some things he or she has overcome? I believe all couples should seek six months of counseling before tying the knot. Interactive counseling will ask the hard questions we are not willing to. As I mentioned before, we are all wearing masks of some kind. We want things to stay hidden. We want to look or be perceived as being better than we are. Sometimes we don't know how to be a wife, husband, mother, father, friend, or any other. The hard questions make us think about who we really are. Choose to be vulnerable and authentic.

Chapter 15

(It's ALWAYS Sunny above the Clouds)
10 Ways to Navigate and THRIVE in Turbulent Times

Creating a checklist for your life

Pilots and flight attendants are given a checklist in an emergency situation. This is for the crew to follow procedure to get the best possible results. We depend on placards and bold faced bullet points the share with the passengers how to follow the plan. These placards highlight the required steps for pilots in the event of an emergency such as fire, or engine failure.

Do you ever notice when you board a plane, that you hear the safety announcement every time? It tells you where to stow your baggage, how to fasten your seat belt, your exit requirements in an emergency evacuation, your personal oxygen for decompression, how to inflate your life vest and rules for the flight.

Many of you that fly frequently, no longer listen to the announcements anymore. Why? You had heard them so much you believe you know them like the back of your hand. When a passenger travels with us for the first time

Chapter 15

they are engaged in the demonstration, they study the placard, look for their life vest and find their nearest exit.

The same thing happens in life. When something is new, we're excited and teachable. When we've done the same thing over and over again, we become complacent and immune. We block out what's important. Become teachable again. Get excited about fulfilling your dream.

This list of 10 ways to THRIVE can be used as your checklist. It's up to you how you use the list. You could have heard some of these things I've spoken about several times, but now is the time to apply it or take action. It's a survival guide to keep you on track. The steps are simple. It may not be easy, just make it worthwhile!

1. Acknowledge & Awareness

Although we have many obstacles to overcome in and our lives, we first have to acknowledge what our shortcomings are. Yes, we all have them. If you still don't know what some of them are, ask some of the people closest to you. Don't take offense, because your objective is to move forward. The only way to do that is to peel the layers away. Acknowledge who you are, where you've been, and where you believe you are going. Think about the positives and the negatives. Take responsibility for your part with what's happened in the past. The sooner we bring it to the light it's easier to move on. What picks you up and what brings you down? Why do you make certain decisions? After acknowledging the issues you have been confronted with it's time to accept what was and what is.

I'll give you an example. I wasn't the best mother I could possibly be over the years. I was too busy "making a living, trying to get ahead." Children need more of our time than anything. I thought if my husband were home, they would get the attention they needed. I was partly right, but I fell short by not giving 100% of myself when I was home. I didn't participate in the PTA, many ballgames, award ceremonies or some of the events that had meaning to them. I felt guilty for years that I'm out of the country almost 15 days a month working.

I acknowledge the fact I made mistakes. For my personal benefit I've written down each area of my life where I may have regrets. We can write down where we lack physically, financially, personally, professionally and emotionally. However, it's easier than you think. This is a step that would be good for you to do. We all have things we'd like to kick ourselves for doing or not doing. I take

Chapter 15

responsibility for my role in it.

This is your first step to healing. It seems too simple, but we understand pain yet sometimes can't recognize symptoms that lead to the pain. It creates an imbalance in our lives so we continue to mask it, because we don't want to be "fixed." It's truly caring enough about you to want to make a change.

We learn the hierarchy of need in which human needs are met. The extreme basic needs are food, water, shelter and oxygen. Then we continue to love, affection, self-esteem, safety and a sense of belonging. This was said by Abraham Madow, these needs are the lowest level that MUST be met before moving to the next step. We can begin with some of the information found above. If you we're not given or shown love or affection, you need to find out what that is and what it means to you. Understand what you know to be true or find people you can emulate. Look for those that have great marriages, those that exude confidence and learn from them.

Awareness is a sense of knowing. It begins when you catch yourself before you say or do something you know you shouldn't do. Let's say you've lashed out in the past to your spouse or friend about what you felt they "didn't" do. This was an expectation you had that they didn't fulfill. The conversation goes south because they can't understand why you are so upset. The next time a situation comes up in the future you are a bit more careful to speak before you react.

You can see throughout the book I'm a work in progress. My husband tells me how easily my words can sound abrupt and demanding. He knows me and understands where I'm coming from, but says he can see when people are offended, when that wasn't my intentions.

Rob and I had an incident in Florida last year which helped me look at things differently. We were furniture shopping and the prices were much higher in that area for used furniture. I'm pretty frugal now so I decided to ask the gentleman working; did they have a clearance section? He looked less than pleased with a scowl on his face and said it's down the road while pointing to the left. I said thanks. My husband and I headed upstairs to see what they had. Rob said the gentleman was being sarcastic, so we decided to go elsewhere. What Rob didn't know, I found out there really was a clearance only store on a recent visit back to Florida. What I learned it's not what we say, but how we

Chapter 15

say it. I could easily tell the man didn't want us to go there and the way it sounded was condescending, however he was truthful. That was a lesson for me in understanding. Our hearts may be in the right place and we're being truthful, but delivery is important.

I'm sure we will all have many circumstances where we took offense to something when it was really nothing. It's so hard for us to look at the best in everyone. We spend a lot of time being in the defensive mode. You know people just don't understand the point you are trying to make. So we defend our statements.

We had friends over recently and played a game we enjoy called Personalogy. This game is supposed to be fun. It really is a lot of fun if you don't really dig into the questions. We have had so many debates about the questions, how we feel or would answer these questions. It comes down to who you are as a person and how confident you are in what you believe. Awareness lets you sit back enjoy friends and family without always injecting what YOU think and believe. People that are still searching for who they are will take your stance or opinion as their truth if they are unsure. Be careful in that arena.

For the example I listed above with my children, I do my best to be as active in their lives as possible. There is not a day that goes by when I'm with them, that I don't tell them how much I love them. I spend time talking to them about what they think and feel. I value their opinions. I want them to know they are important and what they feel matters to me. We discuss how my job has offered them a life most only dream about. It's opened them to seeing how many opportunities are available to them. It's broadened their horizons. I no longer feel guilty. I'm aware that my contribution to their life is just as important.

We are also aware of the fact we don't live in a primitive world any longer. We've evolved over time with newer, easier technology. We finally have electricity, indoor plumbing, telephones and now mobile phones. We no longer have to go kill our food to eat dinner, go milk the cows to have a glass of milk, get the eggs from the chicken to enjoy eggs for breakfast. We have all the modern conveniences our hearts desire. However, it creates one major problem. We have a "microwave mentality" we want results instantly. It takes us years to become overweight, max out credit cards, and have years of false beliefs. Yet we think it should disappear once you understand you have a problem, and take the initial steps in fixing the problem.

It can go as fast as you are willing to put in the time and work. Work seems like a dirty word to most, but I've learned to embrace it. We are not as challenged when we look forward to what's to come.

Bottom line this step will take some time. We don't see our flaws instantly. We don't want to constantly beat ourselves up either. Know that you are important, you matter, you're significant and I believe in you. You can overcome anything you choose.

2. Acceptance

Accept that you're not perfect, you will make mistakes. We're only human. Don't let the inner critic bring more anxiety than what you currently face. Let your emotions go and release what you've kept bottled inside. Cry, scream, yell, and throw a tantrum. You have hidden your imperfections and tried to fit in with the crowd instead of being who you are. It's time to let it go without regret or judgment no matter what you did, or what happened. It doesn't need to stop your progress. You can still do or be anything you choose.

Sometimes we have a hard time accepting others for the way they are. We are all uniquely made. People are wired differently. You may be the type of person that needs to be prompt, likes your home and car clean and tidy. Yet you have a friend that's habitually late, their car or home is a wreck.

You get frustrated because you think they don't have enough respect for you to show up on time. My philosophy is one minute late you miss the plane. I've had to live by that standard for 25 years. My husband is a neat freak, but I've come to like that as well. Before it drove me bonkers, he would have a conniption fit if toothpaste sprayed on the mirror. We used to have friends over and before they are finished with their drinks or food he's picking them up or wiping the counter. It made it annoying having to tell him to stop. It made our friends uncomfortable.

So, what kind of friends do you think I'll attract? You're right, if you said the one's that will challenge me most. Most of them are consistently late. Knowing your friends are like this, tell them to show up and hour earlier. Make adjustments where you can. That was my lesson to have patience and understand everyone is different. I hope you can wrap your head around the fact we need to embrace everyone's uniqueness.

Chapter 15

Another way to acknowledge how you feel about something is to follow it to its root. What I mean by that is when you get angry; ask yourself why? When you follow each question about why you are upset, it more than likely leads to something someone said or did to you in the past. The more questions you ask yourself about why you act or feel what you do come from what we believe or our expectations. The wonderful thing is we have the amazing ability to GET OVER IT. Our pasts are just that in the past. This can only happen when you recognize it. We need to stop looking in the rearview mirror. Focus more on the journey.

The longer I don't accept why I'm negative, controlling, guarded, or whatever the case may be I'll live in misery and want everyone to join me. You've heard that misery loves company. You'll get more of what you are. There is no quality of life in that, if you really want to LIVE! Just as I accept each mistake I've made, I forgive myself and forget it. This is emotional baggage you don't need to carry anymore. Lighten your load, you'll feel better.

I loved the movie "Slumdog Millionaire." It's about a young man that goes on a game show like, who wants to be a Millionaire? What happens is quite fascinating. Each question the young man answered had to do with all of his experiences from the past. The movie would go back in time to explain how he knew the answer to each question. The producers did not believe him, they thought he was cheating.

We all have a rolodex in our brain. We can gather some memories faster than others. Some are triggered by photos, songs or smells. We can pull from childhood memories, people we've met, things we've done, places we've been and so on. They are interconnected someway. This creates links in our chain of life. Each link has significance to us. It doesn't matter how good or bad, happy or sad. Those links are part of who we are. We accept that and continue to move on.

3. Change your thinking

This will be one of the most critical aspects of the ten steps you'll read about. Your life will reveal what you think and believe. So what show's up in your life today? Are you happy with your results? Is you're reality everything you imagined? Most of us have some part of our life we want to change. Some of you may be looking for a clean slate. It's all possible. I'll share a few of the challenges you'll face along the way so it will be an easier transition for you.

Chapter 15

Let's start with how we think and feel about others.

The definition of non-judgment is an observation of people and/or participation in events without imposing our perception, will or criticisms. We grow up learning to judge everyone else. If you're not wearing the right clothes, driving the right car, talking to the right people, listening to the right music, going to the right church than "YOU'RE JUST NOT RIGHT!" We have to catch ourselves daily about what we think or feel about others. This was tough for me. I have been judged my entire life and it was hurtful on many occasions. Through my pain, I did my best to not judge others. I'm human like the rest of you and lashed out many times. I'm not proud of that. It is all part of the lesson.

The fact that we judge something right or wrong doesn't stop people from doing things they would normally do. When we judge them, it's our way of saying that we have placed conditions in loving them. People do what they do based on who they are, what they know and the information they have at the time that supports those beliefs and feelings.

As parents, we impose what we believe as TRUTH on our children. Don't talk to strangers, when the rest of their life they will deal with people. That girl is no good because she comes from THAT part of town, so stay away. We just taught our kids that there is a difference being from the bad part of town. Are they insignificant? Absolutely not! We may tell our kids not to hang around gays or lesbians, blacks or Mexicans which is teaching racism and prejudice. It's our job to LOVE one another and encourage one another. We cannot possibly do this if we are passing judgment on every person we run into. It's still judgment when we are being the FASHION POLICE.

When you learn how to just be, it makes it easier not to judge others. We set an example for people to see what we do in spite of how we feel about it. Decide to take the high road. Judging causes division, animosity and resentment. We can't change minds, we can change hearts. Be open minded, understanding and realize we all have diverse backgrounds and lifestyles. Before you speak put yourself in other's shoes and possibly how they feel about an issue. It's not always about us. That's why we have two ears and one mouth. We should be listening more than we speak. When you point the finger at what everyone else is doing take a look in the mirror, there are more fingers pointed back at you.

Chapter 15

Minding our own business and taking care of us and our families should come first. All beliefs start in the home. Think about any stress related problem you have right now. Does it deal with someone else's business? Are you blaming others for what you don't have? Are you trying to carry the weight of a family member's problem, that's depressing you? Are you lonely, expecting someone to spend time with you? Are you trying to solve your friend's issues? Are you giving advice to others that don't ask for it? Are you an inquiring mind needing to know about what everyone else is doing? Do you feel left out when someone doesn't share their secrets with you? I'm naming a few questions that I've come across just within the last few weeks. They may or may not pertain to you, but think about how some of your stress relates to other people. Eliminate that stress. Think about YOU and how you can help yourself. It is no one person's responsibility to make you happy or feel fulfilled. It comes from within.

I wanted to add a section that I would normally have put into dreams and passions, but it's more appropriate here. When I talk to people about their dreams, I ask one question. If you can be given one thing in life what would it be and why? There are 8 of 10 people that tell me they want a million dollars. I ask, what would you do with it?

Life in the Jetstream

The majority don't have a clue. A few may say a bigger house, nicer car, or pay off some bills, but the vision doesn't go any further. I hope with these statistics below it puts things in perspective.

I learned on my path that we have visions of how millionaires live. We are impressed with Millionaire status as I'll talk about more in finding your passion and living your dreams. Our perception of a Millionaire is most likely different from reality. We think they have the biggest houses, drive the nicest cars, own vacation homes, wear all designer clothes, eat at the fanciest restaurants, and have huge art collections. Do you want to know the truth? Most millionaires' typical annual income is $131,000 up to $247,000 in the 50th percentile. Average net worth is $3.7 million. They live on about 7% of their wealth. Most are homeowners with homes valued at $320,000. Most have lived in those homes almost 20 years. They live well below their means and are extremely frugal. You can read more about them in Millionaire Next Door.

So, basically it's a façade to live up to or try to look like what Millionaire status actually is. That's why it is all smoke and mirrors to try to look the part. People spend what they don't have to look a certain way or to feel well

Chapter 15

accomplished. You can read more in the finance section of this book. I'm bringing this to light here because of how we judge others because of what they have or lack thereof. My perception of a Millionaire came from watching Robin Leach on "Lifestyles of the Rich and Famous." There tag line was Champagne taste with caviar dreams. Boy, it was fascinating, but so unrealistic. I based my truth on this show. How wrong could I be?

When you reach millionaire status, there are no celebrations, fireworks or tingling feelings inside. It doesn't present itself as if you were on a game show being awarded your Million Dollar check. We think of balloons dropping, horns blowing, people cheering about what you've accomplished. The reality is it will be just another day, but don't take that lightly. Every day we can see a beautiful landscape, walk through the grass, visit our family or take another breath, is a blessed day.

We buy into the commercials and marketing being told what everyone has and why we need it. Any company or business that sells you on the need to have more stuff may not be a good fit. It keeps us broke. On the flips side it's not our place to judge the people that can't stop buying. We can share our experiences with our friends and what spending leads to. Ultimately they have to make the decision. Every one of us has a different set of priorities. When you can pay cash for everything, then it's up to you what you do with it. I've lived the hard lesson of financial ruin. I'm grateful for that wake-up call.

Your choice not to judge your family, friends, neighbors, strangers or co-workers depends on you. It's easy to love those that love you back. I am called to love those that are not so easy to love as well. Yes, even when they are mean or rude, even when they gossip or defame you, even when they lie or steal it's not easy, but anything that's worth something of value will not be easy. Your life will uncover peacefulness about you if we can work on this very thing.

De-clutter your life

We have heard this time after time; sometime it takes up to 7 times to hear the same thing for it to sink in. Have you ever noticed how your life seems chaotic sometimes and you don't know why. Take small steps to start the process of cleaning out the clutter everywhere in your life.

What does your car, home, and life say about you? The interesting thing is that I can send a stranger into your

Chapter 15

home without you there, and they can tell me who they think you are. Just by the way your house is decorated, how you organize, how clean or dirty it is, and what your health looks like from the food in your pantry or in the refrigerator. Would you be happy with what information they'd reveal? Why or Why not?

Would you feel like you might have too much work to do to get organized? My husband's birthday gift to me one year was cleaning my closet. Really! I'm still working on this myself. I've learned to let go of many other things and felt the freedom from doing that. Baby steps are good. You have physical clutter in things we give away or sell and we have emotional clutter we rid ourselves of thought patterns.

We started with our cars and cleaned out everything, and then I moved in the house to the main areas where we entertain. I held on tight for years to all the things I thought I needed. It is hard to let go of what we think is sentimental and only to find out why we were keeping it in the first place. That comes from the emotional baggage I carried and what significance I placed on certain things. When I moved out of my dream home in Palm Beach I thought I would be a basket case, yet there was a peace when I left. I knew then it was the right decision. My need to hold on was about what I didn't have growing up. Things were a sign of success to me or what I thought it was. Letting go was difficult. I was used to the chaos and clutter. It was comfortable to me. Are you comfortable in your chaos?

When you see people that have pantries and refrigerators stocked all the time, this shows someone has gone hungry and have the need to keep ENOUGH in case something happens. Basically a good clue is when people overcompensate for their insecurities it will show up somewhere in their life. Ever noticed, someone driving a fancy car and when you finally see their house, it's really small. People want you to see them from the outside only because it's what they lack from within. How are you overcompensating? What can you get rid of? Have a yard sale and raise some money. I'm a fan of craigslist, Facebook Yard Sale Page and Ebay. Try it out for yourself.

When I started getting rid of things, I realized how good it actually felt. I found freedom in letting go, now that I understood why. I will be continuing to simplify my life and de-cluttering areas that don't serve me. Don't just look at material things in your life also look at relationships dragging you down, extra activities that are draining you, and a to-do list you never seem to finish. It's empowering

Chapter 15

to be the person you want to be and NOT what others expect of you.

4. Boundaries

This was a daily learning experience for me a few years ago. I like to say YES to more things than I can personally handle. However, it only wears me out. Are you the same way? A couple years ago I bought the book "The Worn Out Woman" by Dr. Steve Stephens and Alice Gray. A few things got my attention when I saw it in writing. You are controlled by your decisions, not by your circumstances. Do what serves you and where you want to go in life. When you don't have boundaries in your life, people will inject themselves into places in your life where you don't want them. They'll show up in places they have no business being if you allow them.

Imagine a new acquaintance rummaging through your undergarment drawer, or a stranger asking how much do you have in your bank account. Do you have a parent make all your decisions for you at 40 years old, or a co-worker asking to move in for FREE? This may sound outrageous, but every day we don't draw the line where we feel it's being crossed is another day closer to some of these outlandish statements.

You have to filter your input. What are you watching, listening to, seeing on the internet, talking about and thinking about? My husband and I didn't always agree on what TV shows, movies or video games my children could watch or play. I looked at my husband's past and he had both parents still together, he has a great relationship with them, and he didn't get in trouble like I did. I decided to pick and choose my battles. Another reason I agreed to this, is because my husband always seems to explain everything that's right and wrong with a movie and allow my kids to TALK about them openly. I also decided to honor my husband and his decision. You have to choose what to accept for your life.

There are plenty of places to input boundaries with friends, family, business associates, and in every aspect of your life where you can honor yourself. You may say, well I don't want to hurt someone's feelings. Think about the respect you will receive in the long run for standing up for what you believe. Weed out the people in your life that drain your energy. Keep people at arms link that are not going in the direction you want to go. We can't fix everyone's problems, don't loan money unless you don't plan on seeing it again, don't let people borrow things if you are not comfortable with them having it. My rule of

Chapter 15

thumb is if you can't buy it or fix it if something happens to it, DON'T borrow it! Something's seems to magically happen every time it's borrowed.

Boundaries are placed to protect us. It sets the expectation of what you want and believe. What are realistic expectations for you? Let me give you some of my household rules and maybe you can identify in your own situation. Remember, you have your own rules. These are some of mine.

- When we had carpet in our home, we'd need to take off our shoes at the door.
    (Our children lay on the floor to watch TV and I didn't want what was brought in from the shoes.)
- Our children have been required to use their manners. Saying please, thank you yes ma'am yes sir etc. (It's important to show respect.) I have an extremely hard time when kids say yeah what? Or don't even acknowledge you.)
- Turn the lights off when leaving the room you in. (Save energy)
- Everyone has responsibilities around the house. (NO time like the present to learn responsibility.)
- Respect what you have clothing, shoes, electronics

etc. (Let us trust you with what you have and you'll be given more.)
- Don't answer the door if we're not home (Safety is a priority) I can add a few others here, but you can add your own reasons.

- No video games during the week (Only weekends! They don't do it much then either, because they have other things they want to do.)

- We (Parents) will pay for your necessities, but you are responsible for your extra-curricular activities. (If they want the most expensive pair of shoes, a newer electronic, download music, extra items for motorcycles or whatever it may be they have to pay.)

- We don't like calls after 10:00 p.m. (Unless it's an emergency)

I can go on and on with my list, but I want you to get the point of which boundaries you implement for your family.

There are two types of boundaries, physical and emotional. People who have been shamed early in life struggle with creating their own sense of self-worth. They

Chapter 15

don't feel their opinion counts, and what they want is wrong. They grew up with their personal space being violated and felt they weren't important. These emotional boundaries you will need strength to implement.

It gets even worse for those of abuse. Your identity was robbed. Emotional barriers were set up as a self-defense mechanism, just to survive. The unfortunate fact is most of these people tend to attract those that want to control or hurt them. If this is you, notice your patterns and implement some useful boundaries. Understand it's okay to be respected or confront those when they don't. Today is the best time to start learning to trust you.

I went to a workshop in LA years ago. We were able to create a Bill of Rights. These were rights we felt we deserve to live by. Sometimes we are not given a manual on how to live our best life. Create your own Bill of Rights. I'll share a few from my list. Although I filled out two full pages, I want you to have the idea how to do it by yourself and not to let mine influence you.

I have the right to be loved.

I have the right to dream.

I have the right to be valued by my husband and

appreciated by my children.

I have the right to be heard.

I have the right to ask for help.

I have the right to say no.

I have a right to explore new beginnings.

I think it's important to understand how to yield to your rights at times. We can have the expectation of what we want. We as a culture have started a modern day movement to fight for our "rights." The right to vote, the right to equal wages, the right to share household responsibilities, the right to say what we want and do what we want. Holding such demands and fighting for our rights doesn't always bring the promised benefits.

The fact is, happy and successful relationships are not built on demands, but yielding of rights. It's great to create the list of what you want, but it can be turned around in no time. You may decide if your rights are being violated, then you have the right or be angry, frustrated, depressed. Your happiness will be short lived if you are driving on a one way street. If I'm asking for my rights to be met daily and there's the slightest violation, it will leave me feeling uneasy and uptight. Learn to yield your rights and compromise. Relationships are built on love and trust.

Chapter 15

If you don't want people to call you after a certain time make it known. Your family may have an open door policy for people to stop by or NOT. The way you can determine what boundaries you want in place, is by the hesitation or how uncomfortable you feel when someone over steps your personal space. I don't spend much time on social media because it seems to be a way for people to air their dirty laundry. Be Careful!!!! Another thing to remember about social sites: when you react, send nasty messages, you are showing your true character to the world!

You need to put restrictions on social media post. Most adults know what can come back to haunt you in the future, but our children are spinning the wheel of Russian roulette. I can't tell you how many stories I've heard about consequences as a result of what they post. When you are posting a "selfie" that is exposing your body in any way, it's called child pornography. People are posting pictures drinking alcohol, smoking, and rolling joints underage. You see vulgar language and all kind of illegal activity you've now exposed to the world.

Parents talk to your children. Let them know reputations are being made from what they share. Also, when they go for a job interview, the company will have seen the topless photo at Spring break. Companies will look at all social media you have to examine what type of person you are. You may say, "I was just having fun." Posting will cost you in the long run.

Don't let your self-esteem rely on how many "selfies" you take and how many LIKES you get. This is not a personality contest. You could get your feelings hurt more often than not. Don't be something you're not. Don't impress people to be liked, at the end of the day people are watching to see you screw up and then talk about you. The mentality can be cruel. Our children are creating more problems they will eventually have to deal with later. We want to see our children succeed in everything they do, take the time to talk to them and help them understand what can happen.

The best gifts we can give others are encouragement and assistance. We go through life mostly looking out for number one, but we should focus on what we can give in return. It's great to introduce others to our families, friends or contacts that can help them get a new job, a new living situation, a new life experience or even a new love. We treasure the part we played in that role.

Chapter 15

Years ago I'd introduce everyone I know to people that could help further their interests. I needed help along the way and realize how difficult those connections could be sometime. I became more selective later on, because some people just began to burn too many bridges. When cultivating relationships we spend time making sure we honor and respect those people that stay in our lives. When we introduce you to someone of value, we expect you to treat them special. Don't take for granted the relationships or introductions you're privy to because you know someone personally. It's a privilege!

Everything in my being wants to help people pursue their dreams. I'll continue to do that. I wanted to get the point across because so many of us are willing to help you, but we are trusting you to give the same respect to the people we care about. How do people burn bridges? When you ask someone to do you a favor, like a meeting for a new job and you don't show up. You tell someone you will call, and never pick up the phone. You get a service (doctor, dentist, lawyer or chiropractor) from a friend and never pay the bill even though it's discounted. You invite friends to get together for a formal introduction and you show up late, poorly dressed and or intoxicated. Do everyone a favor, don't burn bridges! It's difficult to build them back and causes tension in the relationships. We want to enjoy your new found success and triumphs with you. We want to share our knowledge and blessings with you, if you'll let us.

Boundaries can be broken down simply. Choose to set limits within your comfort zone. Know who you are, what you believe and what you want. Do what serves you? Not in a selfish way, but in your own truth. Learning to say no to more projects and more activities will allow you to visualize what you really want.

5. Forgiveness

I can camp out on this subject for a long time. Years earlier, I realized I had imprisoned myself because I couldn't bear to forgive those who had wronged me. I was the caged animal looking for the way out. We are caged from our pasts or from the expectations of others. We let other people and the past dictate our lives keeping us trapped in a tiny box of beliefs that we cling to.

Let me tell you Forgiveness is a release and the process of letting go. It's removing the errors and judgments from the mind in order to gain happiness and harmony. Many people believe that when you forgive someone, you're doing something for them or maybe letting them off the

Chapter 15

hook. Truth be told, when you forgive, you are doing it for yourself. There is such FREEDOM in forgiving. It's a daily, weekly, monthly and annually process sometimes. Friendships, Relationships can be healed or restored with this one step. Learning how to say I'm sorry or I was wrong will eliminate a lot of stress in your life. You might say but I'm not the one in the wrong. You need to consider, you can always be right or you can be happy, you can't be both. Being right all the time creates a lonely road. It's better to be kind than right. Speak your peace and know you don't have to stay in relationships where you've been wronged.

The way you can decide if you have forgiven someone is every time you think of them you start getting this burning sensation that wells up inside of you. You still have anger or bitterness towards them or you're still out for revenge. It could be as subtle as when you think of them there's dread in your demeanor. We all make mistakes. That's part of life. We need to forgive others or ask forgiveness of those we have wronged or passed judgments on. When I started getting in touch with people I felt I needed to ask forgiveness from, they barely even remembered what I was talking about. It held me in bondage for years, but they had no clue. While you're playing the tapes in your mind over and over again what happened to you, YOU ARE THE PRISIONER. Most people are not giving it a second thought.

Make a choice not to live in bondage. Forgiveness frees you to be who you really are. Something else I learned and shared a bit earlier in the book is that perception can be misconstrued. We all can go to the same party, but if you ask each person that attended: How was the party? You'll get different answers from all of them. One said the party was great and the other said it was boring. You can't convince either to change their mind. Why is that? We all have a different set of beliefs, morals, values and experiences. We also have the right to our opinion. It is the same thing as far as forgiveness. We internalize how we felt about each given situation and decided to get upset, hurt or feeling rejected. This is OUR issue.

We also need to forgive ourselves. The chatterbox on our shoulder tells us how we are not good enough, we're not worthy, we're dumb, who do we think we are, you're a fraud, you're a nobody thinking that you can be SOMEBODY. We have all heard the demeaning voice talking us to a ledge. We believe that voice sometimes and think we'll never be good enough. It's a lie! You do make a difference and you are already SOMEBODY! Forgive

Chapter 15

yourself for your mistakes and shortcomings. Forgive yourself for the way you have been thinking, and forgive yourself that you believed the lies you were told. Many of the lies came from people you respected, admired, look up to, parents, friend's co-workers and many that crossed your path. Turn around and forgive them to. There is POWER that will be restored in you after you forgive.

6. Gratitude

Choices and thoughts are to your soul what food is for your body.

Gratitude is being thankful, counting your blessings, appreciating everything you receive and noticing simple pleasures. The missing ingredient to have a happy, joyful life is to be grateful for EVERYTHING!

How often do we show our gratitude? Not enough! In 2009 I learned why it's so important. I understood giving, serving and compassion, but gratitude is very different. Learning how to be content in all situations brings joy. It made me more positive, more productive, a better wife, mother and friend.

I was introduced to the philosophy to Send Out to Give. Most of us when we send something to someone we expect something in return. It could be a call or a card to say thank you. Something to acknowledge they received it or appreciated it. It was so enlightening when I started sending cards and gifts to people that inspired me or made a difference in my life.

The response I received was humbling. I wrote to teachers, friends and colleagues from years ago. They were excited, appreciative and grateful for such a thoughtful gesture. They had no idea I felt the way I did about them. They made a difference in my life. Who in your life has been there for you? Who has encouraged you? List five people that you'll call or write to this week and tell them how you feel.

There are many benefits to having an attitude of Gratitude. It brings a sense of peace and happiness. It reduces stress, depression, helps you sleep better, strengthens relationships, promotes forgiveness and helps us continue to pay it forward.

Gratitude gives you the quality of life and meaning many of us are searching for daily. Learn how to wake up and be grateful for the gifts currently present in our lives. We take for granted the home we live in, the bed we sleep in, to walk, talk, hear, see, and taste. The clothes we put on, the cars were driving, the food were eating, our health, the things in our home, the modern conveniences we take for granted are part of everything we need to appreciate.

Be conscious to upgrade your level of Gratitude. Find more time in the week to give a compliment, get someone a coffee, bring someone the paper, cook someone a meal, or any small act of kindness to let them know you care. Sometimes just saying thank you for the simple things is enough. It only takes a few minutes.

Learn how to be thankful for your talents, abilities, gifts, resources and anything that makes your life easier. We take for granted the fact we can jump in the car and go to work. What happens if you didn't have the car, or a ride, or money for a taxi? We'd certainly appreciate it and take care of it a bit better. Gratitude attracts more of what we desire. It sends a message that you already have what you desire and therefore open to receive it.

One of the most important lessons that living in gratitude has given me, is an immediate shift in my thought pattern when I'm criticized, upset, start to complain or I'm faced with a major challenge in my life. It takes my mind off me, but gives me the opportunity to grow and learn from each situation.

There is power of having strong relationships. I am so grateful for all of my long-term friendships. I've watched doors open up to things I couldn't imagine through good friends over the years. Recently, our old friends were on Shark Tank. It's my favorite show. Kiowa Kavovit was the youngest entrepreneur at age 7 ever featured on Shark Tank with a product called Boo Boo Goo. It's a paint-on band-aid with various colors that is waterproof. Although filmed in September, it just aired March 2014. It was exciting to see Kiowa's interviews on Good Morning America and in USA Today. Just so you can put a picture with the name, Kiowa is Jen's daughter. Jennifer is being talked about throughout my stories. She married Andrew Kavovit who is an actor and inventor as well. I was so happy for them. They had told us about the product a year before when Kiowa came up with it at 6 years old.

About two weeks later, I get a call from another close friend in LA. Tom is a cosmetic dentist in Beverly Hills. We helped him launch another product called NuBrace at a trade show in Las Vegas years ago. It was about twenty-two years ago I was on the cover of his cosmetic dentist

Chapter 15

brochure. That's how long we've known one another. Tom said he can use our help on his newest product NuPak.

We were at Tom's house last year when he hosted my son and nephew's birthday party celebration. He introduced us to the NuPak in its infancy which is a durable backpack with parabolic inserts that helps support your posture. It's the only technology of its kind. I had my kids try it on and was amazed at the difference. We shot the video and submitted it to Shark Tank. Now I don't know what will happen, but for me it comes down to having genuine, authentic relationships. I'm grateful for the opportunities and the open doors that seem to appear from nowhere. It gives me pleasure to see people I know and love succeed beyond their wildest dreams. Relationships are so important. Take time to build quality relationships.

I'd like you to participate in a 30 day Gratitude Challenge. Who wouldn't want to make someone smile for 30 days? You can see more about this challenge on my website. It's a step-by-step guide how to make a huge impact in another's life. Simply acts of kindness to others allow us to open our hearts and give freely.

7. Giving Back

Living a life of service and compassion will help to bring meaning we desperately seek. With everything I have shared with you thus far, this portion is near and dear to my heart. I included service because it is absolutely a part of having compassion and learning how to give. It took me many years to get over the fact that we should be servants. I took that as a negative connotation. In essence, it's such a GIFT.

The Starfish story has made a tremendous impact on my life. This young boy is out on the beach early one morning. He saw starfish washed up all over the beach. He started picking them up one by one and throwing them in the ocean. A man walking by, said to the boy there are thousands of them, you can't possibly save them all. The boy picked one up threw it in the ocean, and said, "But I saved that one." There are many amazing leaders that made a difference in this world. One person CAN make a difference.

This pulls on my heartstrings, because I look at each starfish as a person. This story has been told for many years, but I have come across hundreds of people hearing it for the first time. What are we doing to help our fellow man? I wanted to give you a few organizations you can start with if you are unsure where to give.

There are so many worthy causes to be a part of. Many challenges society faces are with the struggling economy, poverty, hunger, healthcare and lack of education. Education would be the key to eliminating these problems and be part of the solution. That's how I'm hoping you'll approach giving back. Ask how you can be part of the solution. Don't just give $100 and say I did my part. Think bigger than that. I'm sure they will appreciate your $100, but know there is so much more you can do if you want to.

King's Ransom Foundation: 100% of your money goes directly to the cause. They are dedicated to serving people in need, especially families and children. They support orphans, have helped children be freed from the slave trade, help disaster victim and give clean water. Take time to visit their website. www.kingsransomfoundation.org

KIVA: $25 gives someone in a third world country an opportunity to start a business. They pay it back. $25 for a CHANCE an Opportunity we are freely given every day. www.kiva.org

Make A Wish Foundation: Check out a near and dear

friend's story about his personal journey with Make A Wish Foundation. He was given a wish and gave it to someone else who eventually lost their battle. Tyler Ganus has fully recovered and is raising $10,000 to create a wish for another worthy recipient. www.makeawish.org

GIVE BLOOD: check your local blood bank. I didn't realize how important this was. In the midst of disaster we run to give blood, but there's a need year around. Also if you are a rare blood type as mine, give at least once a year. I made the excuses I don't like needles, but I can put on my big girl panties for a few minutes to help a cause.

Big Brothers Big Sisters: a mentoring organization for children with single parents. Look up your local chapter www.bbbs.org

St. Jude Children's Research Hospital: The mission is to advance cures and means of prevention. No child is denied treatment on race, religion, or a family's ability to pay. www.stjude.org

Tithe: Give to your local church organization. Give 10% of your income and offering is anything above that. You can do that with the church you attend on a regular basis or through organizations that are care for the needy, homeless,

Chapter 15

widows etc.

You can see my extensive list on the website at www.resultdrivenlife.com

List of ways to give back for FREE or very little:

Volunteer at a nursing home

Pay someone's toll

Donate old books

Smile it's contagious

Compliment someone

Anticipate needs of others

Bring coffee to a co-worker

Send a card or flowers to someone going through a hard time.

Remember birthdays (if yours is important so is theirs)

Pay someone's parking meter

I love the quote from Marianne Williamson's book, "The Healing of America." The fabric of American society must be rewoven one loving stitch at a time: one child read to, one sick person prayed for, one elder given respect and made to feel needed, one prisoner rehabilitated, and one mourner given comfort. The idea is to start somewhere.

8. Write It Down & Finding Your Why

Writing our thoughts, feelings, goals and dreams on paper make it real. Some of you will feel the need to skip this part so I'd like to offer a challenge for those willing to participate. We will follow up through my website to see how the experiment unfolds.

I have hundreds of notebooks I've filled over the years. I have kept many of them just to look and see where I was at the time of my writing. Can you imagine looking back at your dream and goal list only to find they ALL came true? I'll give you a few examples because I had no idea they could happen to me.

- I wanted my husband to be a stay at home dad. Everyone said it couldn't be done.
- I wanted 2 homes, my home and a vacation home.
- I wanted to be a real-estate investor. I learned to buy, sell and remodel homes.
- I wanted 3 vacations a year. This is not as important to me now, because I vacation while doing the things I love, so I'm on a permanent vacation.
- I wanted to have six figures in the bank. When you are raised poor, been in financial ruin, it seems money is the only security. It's NOT!

Chapter 15

These were written over many years. I knew my history and thought these things were too impossible. It was bleak, but looking back at my many lists THEY HAPPENED! It's REAL.

I have surpassed every dream I have put on paper. However, I'm starting a new list.

Writing makes your feelings more like speed bumps instead of roadblocks. Speed bumps may slow you down, but don't completely stop you. It helps you process information and become clear on what you want.

Another important reason to put your thoughts on paper is to identify the value of words. There is a book called *The Dream Giver*, by Bruce Wilkinson. It talks about a place called Land of Familiar where many Nobodies live. There are nobodies that want to be somebody soon. There are several obstacles they face here to get through before they ARRIVE to their DREAM. It's not easy, but it's attainable. You must read it. I also came across a poem soon after reading *Dream Giver*. I thought it was appropriate to share. It's called "Leaving the City of Regret."

Leaving the City of Regret
by: Larry Harp

I had not really planned on taking a trip this time of year, and yet I found myself packing rather hurriedly. This trip was going to be unpleasant and I knew in advance that no real good would come of it. I'm talking about my annual "Guilt Trip."

I got tickets to fly there on Wish I Had airlines. It was an extremely short flight. I got my baggage, which I could not check. I chose to carry it myself all the way. It was weighted down with a thousand memories of what might have been. No one greeted me as I entered the terminal to the Regret City International Airport. I say international because people from all over the world come to this dismal town.

As I checked into the Last Resort Hotel, I noticed that they would be hosting the year's most important event, the Annual Pity Party. I wasn't going to miss that great social occasion. Many of the towns leading citizens would be there.

First, there would be the Done family, you know, Should Have, Would Have and Could Have. Then came the

Chapter 15

I Had family. You probably know ol' Wish and his clan. Of course, the Opportunities would be present, Missed and Lost. The biggest family would be the Yesterday's. There are far too many of them to count, but each one would have a very sad story to share.

Then Shattered Dreams would surely make and appearance. And It's Their Fault would regale us with stories (excuses) about how things had failed in his life, and each story would be loudly applauded by Don't Blame Me and I Couldn't Help It.

Well, to make a long story short, I went to this depressing party knowing that there would be no real benefit in doing so. And, as usual, I became very depressed. But as I thought about all of the stories of failures brought back from the past, it occurred to me that all of this trip and subsequent "pity party" could be cancelled by ME! I started to truly realize that I did not have to be there. I didn't have to be depressed. One thing kept going through my mind, I CAN'T CHANGE YESTERDAY, BUT I DO HAVE THE POWER TO MAKE TODAY A WONDERFUL DAY. I can be happy, joyous, fulfilled, encouraged, as well as encouraging. Knowing this, I left the City of Regret immediately and left no forwarding address. Am I sorry for mistakes I've made in the past? YES! But there is no physical way to undo them.

So, if you're planning a trip back to the City of Regret, please cancel all your reservations now. Instead, take a trip to a place called, Starting Again. I liked it so much that I have now taken up permanent residence there. My neighbors, the I Forgive Myself's and the New Starts are so very helpful. By the way, you don't have to carry around heavy baggage, because the load is lifted from your shoulders upon arrival. God bless you in finding this great town. If you can find it, it's in your own heart, please look me up. I live on I Can Do It Street.

Finding your why is significant. It will be the only thing that gets you up in the morning, every morning. I call it the "Why" that makes you cry. Think about how you want to design your life. Why does that matter to you? If you do not have an emotional reason to keep you focused on a better life, it will be easy to quit and mold to society. What makes your heart hurt? Most of us ride this life by the seat of our pants. We start by asking ourselves, what do I want in life? Then we say, how can I get that? We are more familiar with logic than discovering where the drive will come from. If you don't know your why, more than likely you will be constantly searching. I heard a great quote. "Keep your eye on the why, the what doesn't matter and the how will show up."

9. Finding your passion and living your dreams!

I think that we believe a purpose will give our lives meaning, will make us feel special or more important and will give us permission to express our hidden passions. What exactly is purpose and passion? Purpose seems to come from a personal experience where we become focused and determined to accomplish something. Your purpose can be feeding the hungry, creating environmentally safe products, taking care of the elderly or just being a loving person. Our purpose has been lying dormant within us for years. It's time to dust off the cobwebs and figure it out.

Do you have something you love to do? Do you want to make money doing it? I shared some of my story earlier in the book. I had a love for charity work. If money were no object that's all I would be doing. I have been super blessed to work with many charities and people in need. I thought making money to GIVE to the charities was how I would see my vision through, but it wasn't. God said to me, why do you keep waiting on what I've called you to do? You

Life in the Jetstream

can start right now. I didn't see that coming. We wait till we have the better job, the amount of money we think we need, and raise the children before we start living on purpose.

I wanted to work it out logically in my brain, how all of this would come into fruition. It doesn't work that way. When I was only 4 years old during Christmas, I was told I would be going into the Public Relations field because I wanted to help everyone. That was a sign. I was talking to my husband recently about dreams. I was explaining we can have a dream to build orphanages, he immediately says but that's not my dream. I told him I know that. I was merely making a comment because his dream is NOT my dream. We all have our very own DREAM within us.

Passion is the spark, the motivation the drive behind a purpose. Having passion takes away the sense of obligation of a purpose. Picture a car. You need fuel to go anywhere (passion) and you need a key to start the motor (purpose.) Now you are in the driver's seat and can easily use these tools constructively or destructively. It's up to you! I love that! This was stated from Rhonda Britton author of Change your life in 30 days. The downside is how we get addictions. When we are in pursuit of our passion and

Chapter 15

purpose we sometime fall short from rejection, and missed opportunities. Then the risk no longer seems worth it.

I love the quote that says "You don't always get what you wish for; you get what you work for." You have to be driven to fight for what you want in life. Let's say that you are not so sure what your purpose is, or what dreams you may have, it's only a matter of time. Start writing down everything you like, enjoy, feel you are good at and can speak passionately about. It's important to differentiate between goals and challenges. A goal can be an item on your to do list or checklist. Challenges are something that stretches your efforts, talents or abilities. This is why we need to focus on the journey not the destination.

About 4 years ago I was talking on the phone with one of my closest friends. Erik is someone I met over twenty two years ago on the "Power Ranger" show. You remember the one, the Mighty Morphin Power Rangers that kids would just flip over, literally. I use to do extra work on the show and I got to know all of the cast members. We had many great times together. Erik is what I call one of my growth friends. When we talk, it's always about moving forward, buying houses, investment ideas, economics, the acting business, and the list goes on.

I recall one particular conversation. I was standing outside beside the pool at my friend's house in Bel-Air. We normally go out to Los Angeles for a few weeks during the summer. I'm not sure how we got on the subject, but we were talking about my mentors. He asked what I saw in them that I didn't see in myself. We're faced with insecurities and I'm no different than everyone else. I was talking about my fear of public speaking. As I said before, my mentors are Dani Johnson and Ellen Ganus. They're both amazing coaches, well accomplished business developers and leaders, authors, speakers, philanthropist, loving wives, mothers and life changers.

I proceeded to tell Erik what I thought my inadequacies were. He said you know what amazes me? I said what. He said I see all of those qualities in you already and you can't even see it in yourself. You have the same gift if you only choose to walk in those shoes. He said the next time you are offered a speaking engagement, TAKE IT! What do you have to lose? Believe it or not it was only a few months later I was asked to speak at a Women's Conference at a local Museum. I said yes. That was monumental for me. I had the experience talking to people one-on-one, but speaking in a group terrified me. It reminded me of the book "Feel the fear and Do it anyway." by Dr. Susan

Jeffers. It was definitely Erik's belief in me that I already was that person. I could do it.

Finding your why will break it down for you. Your challenge is to find what makes you feel most alive. What drives you or gives you great satisfaction. Don't think about what you fear in pursuit of your dream. Don't think about the failures you had before. Start defining who you are today, and what you want to become. Stop living in your past, but rather start living into your future. Think about all of the possibilities you have, not the pitfalls.

Next you need to clarify what it is you want and how to accomplish it. If I asked you the question right now, what do you want to accomplish in your life? What would you say? Write it down. I've covered the importance of put it in writing. Seriously! Write it down and date it.

Unfortunately, most of us don't have the foggiest idea of what we want. Decide to create a detailed vision or what you want to accomplish. It is all in the action steps you take that moves you to your goal. Clarify the vision in all aspects of your life physically, financially, spiritually, and mentally. Visualize being where you want to be; having what you want and doing the things that seem impossible. I admire the actor Jim Carrey. He wrote himself a 10 million dollar check and kept it in his wallet for years. He gave himself a specific date to reach the goal. Here's a guy riding around in a broken down car, sitting on Mulholland Drive visualizing that he already hit his goal. It didn't matter how much rejection he faced, he already knew it would happen for him. It was three years to date he made his 10 million dollar check for Dumb and Dumber.

Know your deepest darkest desires and figure out why you have that desire. You'll fight a tough fight only for something you believe in. This becomes your Why? What makes you want to get out of bed every morning? What drives you to keep going when you feel like giving up? What keeps you pushing through the barriers, when everyone is telling you, you can't? Having the courage to pursue you dream can be risky, yet honorable. It will scare you, yet bring out the best in you. Your dream could be the best mother and wife you can possibly be. It doesn't mean you have to save the world, climb Mt. Everest or feed the hungry. Being the best wife and mother is a GREAT DREAM!

Here's the other option. Take the road heavily traveled. Declare you don't have a dream, no desires, no aspirations and no purpose. If you continue to do non-productive things like watch more television, stayed hooked social media by the minute, play more mindless games to pass time and keep hanging out with negative people. This will keep you stagnant and will produce no results in your life. Your environment regulates your circumstances. I will go ahead and address the feedback I'll receive about this paragraph. I covered a section about not being judgmental. I mean that with all of my being. However, I don't judge you personally. When people ask me for help, they are explaining what they do. What you do in your spare time tells me how to help you with your problem. The actions listed above are many reason's people don't fulfill their purpose.

When I'm working on one of my various projects, I constantly hear people tell me I would just love to do what you do. I'm flattered. My response back to them is why are you not doing it? I'm amazed at the excuses I hear. I am honest and upfront with them, if it's something you want to do, DO IT! I too, waited for some of the things I thought I couldn't do. I want to live without regret. When I see their eyes light up and their voice raises out of excitement, they are hanging on my every word, I know they have a DREAM!

I love seeing that kind of spark in people, it means they are ALIVE! I have always been someone that goes from A to Z. I get so many ideas, but I go from the idea to the finished company in no time. This would drive my husband berserk! It would frustrate him to no end. He thinks if you don't hit all the letters, the foundation will not be solid. Follow me here. That can be true, but the disheartening thing is most people give up before they get to letter E because of the opposition that comes your way. If you can finalize your vision with and ending in mind, it's easier to stay focused on the goal. You can have small goal or large ones it's up to you. What I do know is they need to be specific. We've been taught to do things backwards. Start a project and see how it unfolds. Not exactly! What is the final dream and results you'd like?

Let me give you an example of a basic goal versus a specific goal. This one is typical and I'm sure you've heard it before. There's a woman who wanted so badly to be a millionaire. (GOAL) She works hard, stays focused and gets the million dollars at all cost. She loses her family, her health, and her real passion. She did get what she asked for didn't she? Now let's say I want to have a three-hundred thousand dollars in my bank account in ten years, but I don't want to get stuck doing things I don't love, like

Chapter 15

administrative work, sitting at a desk or hard labor. I want to be fit and healthy and keep my family close to me. I want to enjoy the people I work with. I want to have several growth friends to toss around ideas. (SPECIFIC GOAL) This may not be your goal, but it gives you a starting point to work with. It doesn't matter how big or small your vision is, what's important is that you get started.

You might think your dreams are meaningless right now, but there's power in believing and seeing it on paper. It can be a way to part from your worries and fears. You have to take small steps before you can crawl, walk or run. Nothing will happen when you generalize or use blanket statements. When you stay safe, nothing will change in your life. List your intentions and be specific. Design a vision board. Pick 5 or 6 things you'd like to accomplish this year. Put them on poster board. Tear photos from magazines, print pictures from the internet, write words that move you. I've used quotes and words that I'll share with you.

"I am the author of my own life." "You must be the change you want to see in the world," Gandhi. "In the middle of difficulty lies opportunity." Einstein. "The future belongs to those who believe in the beauty of their dreams."

Eleanor Roosevelt. "I am divinely guided and protected." Some of my words are believe, faith, hope, celebrate, imagine, create and courage.

Growing up with a life of dysfunction, I am still so blessed beyond compare. Who would have thought a girl from the other side of the tracks could" LIVE HER DREAM." My suffering has brought me strength, determination and perseverance. I CHOOSE not to be a victim of circumstance. I choose to live a life of meaning and purpose. I grew up with abuse, bullying, and violent fights in the home, suicide, drugs and alcohol, getting shot, financial ruin among so many other issues. I still managed to get back up and brush myself off and keep going. YOU CAN TO! It's not too late.

10. Living the Dash

I wanted to end with living the dash to give you a whole new perspective. I've come across this concept many times and it has more of an impact each time I've read it. Imagine you are given six months to live. Time is of the essence. How would your life be different? What would you change?

Now that you know you're dying in six months, what is

Chapter 15

the first thing you'd do? Who would you tell? Will you tell anyone? Will you take the trip you've always wanted to take? Will you live without fear having to please everyone? Would you work less? Would you spend time with those you love? Will you get closure from family and friends and tell them how you really feel? So many questions so little time. The choice is in your hands.

You can make this a bit more real by writing your obituary. So many people avoid this subject. Why do we not want to accept that we will pass on? It's only a matter of time. Be prepared; don't let your family carry the burden. While I'm talking about this, please take the time to wrap up your affairs. I've watched many estates no matter how large or small go into probate because people don't want to talk about dying. It will happen. Get your wills and trusts taken care of now.

Let family know what your final requests are when you pass on. Do you want to be buried or cremated? Do you want a wake, funeral or a party? My intention is not to bring you down, but help you prepare for the inevitable.

Life is too short. Our time on earth is limited. Dying is inevitable, but truly living is up to you. So, what does

"Living the Dash" mean? Your tombstone will read your name, the date you were born, the dash in between and the date you died. The dash signifies how you lived while you were here. What kind of impact did you make? What legacy did you leave?

Prioritize your life starting today. "There" is no better than "here." I am one that likes to make TO DO list and check them off to see how much I could accomplish, like Wonder Woman. For years I wore myself out trying to accomplish such tasks. One day I looked at some of these lists and I laughed. I wrote every detail and still do, but what's different is I only do what is a priority that day or week. I do what I choose to do today. I'm not on a mission anymore to say I did it all. Nobody cares at the end of the day. One of my favorite quotes is "Nobody cares about the storms you've encountered, but did you bring in the ship?" Life is going to be rough; you will have hardships, and heartbreak. People only care if you overcame it and did something about it.

When I was living in Florida I was on a path to make a lot of money thinking that's what I was supposed to do. I spent a lot of time networking, doing seminars, participating at festivals and spending time in my office

Chapter 15

shuffling papers and dialing for dollars. I was in the back office in my Palm Beach home calling new clients.

I guess I started doing dishes when I had a return phone call in my office. I ran for the phone. I spent quite some time on this business call. I'm hearing the dripping of water and wondering what it is? I walked into my open floor plan kitchen and living room and I see water all over the floor running everywhere. I had to jump off the phone to take care of the flood. I realized I left the faucet running when I ran for the call.

My husband was a police officer at the time and he was sleeping. I was scurrying around to quickly clean up the mess. I had about ten towels in the floor. I wiped down the cabinets and tried to make it spic and span before he woke up. I threw the towels in the bathroom tub that he never goes into. I was relieved when I finished. He wakes up and walks in the room. I act as if everything was NORMAL. He sits on the couch and sees water going out by the 3 sliding glass doors and asked: What is that? He wakes up and sees something so small abnormal. I said nothing or I don't know. He decides to get up to go in the kitchen and get a spoon for his coffee and it was then I was found out. The entire draw was FULL of water and went all over the floor.

339

I put my head down because I knew he was going to be very upset with me because this was just ONE of the times I was not PRESENT.

I had two small children at the time who knew mommy was always on the phone, always in the office, always going to meetings and for the most part not present. I may have been there physically, but certainly not mentality. I went through the motions. I didn't know how to be a mother, a wife, or friend. I followed in my mother's footsteps to work hard and be busy. I thought that's the way it was. I thought I was working to give my family a better future. However, I was losing what I wanted most because of my need to be challenged. I spent my days trying to hit insignificant goals, that my children were growing up and I wasn't really there. Absentee parents are harming the next generation just as much as the single-parent. Children need good influences. They can care less about the stuff you have and how much you earned. What's important is did you care and participate in their life.

We spend our life saying if I could just turn 16, 18, or 21. If I could have a great job, if I could get married, if I just had more money, if I had a college degree, if I had a better car, a nicer house, or whatever it may be we'd be

Chapter 15

happy. We waste so much energy trying to be somewhere else then enjoying where we are right now. There is a gift in everyday circumstances if we are just present. However, to live in the future of what you want will only leave you empty because of what you miss out on today.

One of the greatest gifts you can actually give yourself is personal growth. I'm not talking about getting motivated for a few days. It's time to get connected to a source. Plug in to all aspects of your life. Prayer and Meditation is your friend. I love analogies and have learned from them quite often. It helped me understand the importance of being connected and plugging in.

Think about the lamp beside your bed. It's nighttime, you can't see so you flip the switch to turn it on and NOTHING happens! You check the light bulb is tight and still NOTHING. Then you hit the shade and flip the switch on the wall and you still don't have light. You're confused and wonder why it's not turning on. Something is wrong with this light. Finally, you look at the plug and realized someone else must have UNPLUGGED it! We still don't get it sometimes. The only way to learn and grow is to get plugged into a source of information.

I constantly feed my mind positive influences. I read books or listen to conference calls. I watch things that will help me grow online whether it's a great leader, a sermon, reading about finances and what's changing for entrepreneurs. I'm researching and looking for things of interest. I'm constantly gathering new information. There is power in getting plugged in.

We want to get physically fit, yet we don't go to the gym or eat better. We want to get spiritually connected yet we don't go to church, read the bible, meditate, or pray. We want to clean up our emotional baggage, but we don't want to relive the painful past and do the work that will get us through. We want to be financially free, yet we are not willing to stop spending. You have to decide when enough is enough. Are you sick and tired of being sick and tired? Excuses are not an option. We don't get what we want in our life because we've decided the sacrifice is too much. We get what we want because in the end we know it's worth it!

In this day and time we have so much information it can be an overload. If you want something to change in your life, you have to be open and willing to PLUG IN! Be consistent in all that you do. Decide what you want to

Chapter 15

change and like Nike says, JUST DO IT!

Living the dash reminds us to live now. Don't wait on what may or may not come. Think about how you want to be remembered. What kind of mark did you make? Did you leave the world a better place than you found it? Did you love others? Did you find out what matters most to you? These are questions you'll ask yourself in the end. The other "stuff" doesn't have a place in your life when you know your life is coming to an end.

I promise your life will be more abundant and fulfilled by learning to live as if you were dying. When you know that these are your last days it creates a sense of urgency. You prioritize differently. Look around at some family and friends that left this world way too soon. We want to have a moment in time to say the things we wanted to say or do what we wanted to do with our loved ones. We look back and regret that which we did not do. You have tools at your fingertips to use any way you choose. Choose to truly live and love. Choose to be the light and make a difference in the world around you.

Living a "Life in the Jetstream" signifies people living their dream, yet navigating the course when life happens.

Life in the Jetstream

We have reached our final cruising altitude. (Living your dream) You are now free to roam about the cabin. (Make decisions and accept challenges) However, we may hit turbulence and encourage you to keep your seatbelt fastened when you are seated. (Stay focused on your goal even through the obstacles) We have approximately 14 hours and 15 minutes to our destination. (Time is limited.) Sit back and relax and enjoy the ride. (It's YOUR journey to do as you please.)

Are you ready to live your "Life in the Jetstream?" Better yet, ready to live YOUR dream!